DESIGNED BY ADVENTURE

DESIGNED BY ADVENTURE

30 YEARS OF
OUTDOOR RESEARCH

Topher Donahue

RMB

Rocky Mountain Books
www.rmbooks.com

Library and Archives Canada Cataloguing in Publication

Donahue, Topher

   Designed by adventure : 30 years of Outdoor Research / Topher Donahue.
ISBN 978-1-926855-82-0

   1. Outdoor Research (Firm)—History. 2. Sport clothes industry—Washington (State)—Seattle--History. 3. Sporting goods industry—Washington (State)—Seattle—History. I. Title.

HD9948.5.U64O98 2011   338.7′68716   C2011-906158-9

Cover photo by Jason Hummel. *Outdoor Research Ambassador Tom Murphy, Jessy Hummel and Adam Roberts skinning on the Isolation Traverse in the North Cascades, Washington.*

Printed in The United States of America

Contents

1

The Free Climbing Revolution

We are drawn to adventurers and to adventure stories because they tell us what we forget: that each of us is on an adventure, that our lives are filled with opportunities to wake up and do the right thing – that we'll know that right thing when we allow ourselves to see it.

— Clint Willis, *Adrenaline 2002*

RON GREGG JAMMING IN THE BIG OFFICE, MONTE CRISTO, WASHINGTON.

Thirty years ago, the mountaineers and climbers who had the best gear were the ones who made their own. Backpacks didn't have long enough straps to hold anything, so extensions were stitched onto the packs' accessory straps. Climbing harnesses didn't come with gear loops to hold carabiners and other equipment, so many climbers added their own. Mountaineers sewed ice axe holsters onto the waist belt of their harnesses and backpacks so they could easily store or pull out the tool. Ice axe leashes were nearly useless – they fell off wrists, making it easy to lose the tool, or they worked like a tourniquet on climbers' circulation if they hung from them on steep terrain – so almost everyone had a homemade or modified leash.

A climber in Colorado made an entire kit of camouflage outerwear and a matching backpack. His motivation was one part a desire to have gear that worked better than what was available at the time, and one part a habit of camping without a permit in a National Park before doing big climbs. He later went on to work as a law-enforcement ranger.

Even the generally law-abiding often sported customized equipment. The more out-there the adventure, the more the gear had to be customized and made by hand. Nearly every big wall and big mountain climber had modified gear. Haul bags were usually handmade entirely or pieced together with seatbelts from the junkyard sewn onto army surplus duffel bags. When big wall climbers grew tired of sleeping in shoulder-crunching hammocks for camping on sheer rock walls, they built the first portaledges by using webbing tied to full-length lawn chairs. In the mountains, climbers modified jackets so the hoods fit over helmets, and stitched gauntlets onto their gloves to keep the snow out of them for alpine and ice climbing. Eerie body-bag-looking sleeves were sewn onto backpacks to create makeshift bivouac sacks. Anything metal that was deemed too heavy was taken to a friendly machine shop where the climbers would drill the overweight piece full of dozens of holes to lighten the load.

Every mountaineering community revered the locals who had the right tools for modifying gear. A climber named Mike Caldwell, the father of the now-famous Yosemite free climber Tommy Caldwell, had an industrial sewing machine and a metal shop in his garage.

Mike would show up for a climb with nearly every piece of his kit customized to some degree. Rock climbers had stopped using hammers and pitons by then, but he welded a small hammerhead onto his cleaning tool for testing old fixed pitons, and created a gear racking system with Velcro tabs to facilitate the fastest access to a crucial piece. Chalkbags – little bags of gymnastics chalk – became popular for rock climbing in the 70s, but the available designs were so bad that Mike made his own, complete with spill-proof closures, flashy colors and a reinforced opening that allowed for quick access even in the most desperate moments. And not only that, he carried one on each hip so he didn't have to reach so far for a refreshing dip.

The need for more sophisticated gear wasn't isolated to specialized mountaineering and rock climbing. Everyone who recreated in the mountains got wet feet, fiddled too much with their equipment and eventually started thinking about how things could be better. Nobody cared what gear looked like. In fact, the more wildly colored and obvious a gear modification was, the more street cred you got. Today, if you showed up at the ski area with gloves sporting a homemade gauntlet sewn out of bright-orange nylon, you'd be the biggest dork on the hill. In 1981, though, skiers would have been offering to buy those gloves right off your hands.

By the 70s, mountaineering was already a well-established endeavor, with Reinhold Messner and Edmund Hillary being household names worldwide, but it was the invention of free climbing that changed everything. Many non-climbers still think free climbing suggests climbing without a rope, where a fall means certain death. In fact, the sport is quite the opposite. The "free" part means that you attempt to climb the rock without suspending your weight on ropes or equipment. The duality of the challenge of free climbing, within the relative safety of a properly managed rope system, made it a relatively easy and safe way to get into mountain sport. Free climbing allowed the popularity of climbing to grow by leaps and bounds, eventually inspiring climbing gyms and organized competitions and turning the world of mountaineering into a mainstream adventure sport. University outing clubs added rock climbing to their programs. Innovators began making outdoor equipment that was designed for adventure, and the world of mountain sport became much more appealing to many more people.

In alpine mountaineering, improved technology and the free climbing ideal of going faster, lighter and under human power were changing the game as well. It was all about doing more radical things with less equipment and less impact on the mountain. In 1976, the highest peak in North America, Alaska's 20,320-foot Denali (called Mt. McKinley for many years, before being officially changed back to Denali, the peak's native name) was climbed alpine style. Alpine style, for those unfamiliar with mountaineering's way of differentiating a game without written rules, essentially means getting up the mountain without fixing ropes in place or doing extensive route preparation. Alpine style was allowing faster ascents of more difficult and dangerous climbs. Gear innovations and attitude changes were allowing not just slight improvements in the sport, but quantum leaps.

Climbers like Jeff Lowe and Yvon Chouinard were designing technical tools with the goal of pushing the cutting edge of mountaineering, but much of the most basic equipment was laughable. Everyone who explored the mountains, including hikers, skiers and mountaineers, learned quickly that the best gear of the day worked only in the mildest of conditions – if at all.

"Waterproof and breathable" was a contradiction in terms. Gaiters were supposed to keep sand and snow out of your boots,

OUTDOOR RESEARCH AMBASSADOR HANS JOHNSTONE CLIMBS, WITH THE BENEFIT OF GEAR OPTIMIZED FOR PERFORMANCE BY DECADES OF REFINEMENT, ON THE BECKEY ROUTE, SOUTH FACE OF THE GRAND TETON, WYOMING.

but they didn't. Instead, they often funneled the stuff directly into your boots. They worked alright for keeping dust and small rocks out while hiking dusty trails in the summer, but the winter was a different animal. A common winter scene on the trail was a guy sitting on his pack cleaning pounds of snow out of his gaiters. Everyone hated them. Climbers pushed the limits of what they could do without them simply because the gaiters of the day worked about as well as a wet towel wrapped around each leg. Gloves were even worse. They weren't waterproof, didn't fit and were unusable for any activity requiring dexterity. Leather and Gore-Tex ski gloves were common, but they were bulky, dried slowly and were not really designed to allow the finger coordination required for handling climbing equipment.

At that time, the best system for keeping your hands warm while mountaineering was a thin, skin-tight silk glove worn inside a heavy, spun-wool mitten called the Dachstein mitt. The system was a pathetic excuse for extreme weather wear but it was the best thing going. For harder climbing or anything requiring dexterity, you wore the glove and left the wool mitten hanging around your wrist from a home-sewn strap. The mittens caught on everything and filled up with snow, but when you put them back on, the heat from your hands – provided you had any left – melted the snow, the wool wicked the moisture away and you soldiered on, dreading the next time you had to take your mittens off.

Most of these gear builders stayed in the closet, but a few decided to sell their inventions and ultimately helped shape the world of modern mountain adventure. It was an exciting time to be a mountaineer with a penchant for design and an obsession with function. One of these innovators, a man who couldn't resist the fundamental idea of making outdoor equipment better, was Ron Gregg, an energetic physicist from the Pacific Northwest.

Watching this sea change happen as an avid young adventurer would have been an inspiring spectacle. As a physicist and a tenacious critic of all things imperfect, Ron immediately determined that the equipment available was far from acceptable. He would also have seen that, from the highest peaks to the steepest walls, the once lunatic-fringe world of mountain adventure was becoming more fun, thanks in no small part to the combined contributions of these closet innovators.

Research was ingrained in his insatiable psyche from the beginning. With an IQ of 200, Ron skipped third grade and went on to graduate as valedictorian of his high school class at age 16. The brilliant mind of the young man was so distracting for him that athletics held little interest until he discovered the intellectual world of mountain sport.

School was easy for him and he couldn't get enough. The summer after his junior year of high school, he spent six weeks at science camp studying calculus and physics. By his senior year, Ron had already aced all the math classes available, so he attended the local community college for math. Classical music appealed to him, so he learned violin, playing first chair through his school years and then in the orchestra during college.

Growing up on the water of Lake Washington, north of Seattle, Ron was an avid water skier and sailor at a young age, with an energetic streak that left friends and family rocking in his wake in everything he did. Even after he discovered the thrills of international mountaineering, his enthusiasm for smaller adventures never diminished. His sister, Laurie Nicol, recalls that anytime they were both at the family house on Lake Washington, he would come into her room early in the morning and literally carry her outside so they could ski while the water was still glassy smooth.

It was during undergraduate studies at Caltech that Ron first explored human-powered mountain sports on rock climbing trips with the university outing club. With a sturdy physique, tenacious mental endurance and a stubborn streak from the day he was born, he was magnetically attracted to rock climbing – and he was good at it. Besides the obvious joys of playing in some of the world's most spectacular natural sporting arenas, there was the intellectual element of rock-climbing equipment and problem solving that fit the physicist's mind like a well-designed glove.

Once Ron had fallen in love with rock climbing, it wasn't long before running rivers and climbing mountains pulled him under the beguiling spell of human-powered gravity sport. Considering his physics aptitude, and the unrefined state of outdoor products at the time, if he could have seen his future he might not have been surprised to know he would one day be drawing lines on his hand so he could visualize a shaped glove that would make holding ice axes and ski poles easier.

By the time free climbing caught on in the 70s, other outdoor sports, including surfing and skiing, were already considered hip, thrilling and athletic ways to find challenge and excitement in the natural environment. Mountain sport was a more slowly acquired taste for the mainstream palate. And Ron liked it fine that way and it showed in his personal style. By his assessment, jeans and a tank top were just about the only clothes a man should ever need in the city; only the orchestra was worth dressing up for. Plus he sported a sturdy moustache that only accentuated his already razor-sharp opinions, inspiring his future wife, Sharon, to quip, "It makes you wonder if he was born with that moustache."

It wasn't until the information revolution that people from all walks of life decided they wanted to taste the adventure experience themselves – and the popularity of mountain sport exploded. Throughout the most transitional decades of the popularization of adventure sport, Ron was one of a small handful of innovators that helped make human-powered recreation in the wilderness as popular, fun and safe as it is today. By 2011, backcountry skiing would be the fastest-growing outdoor sport in America and the combined economic heft of the outdoor industry would be nearing a trillion dollars annually. In the long run, making outdoor adventure more fun made it appealing to more people and gave rise to an industry which continues to be a prosperous, healthy, growing and inspiring place to work and play. All it took was a short stint as a nuclear physicist and a life-changing expedition to Alaska to derail Ron Gregg's lofty career track and give him and his adventures a legendary role in designing the future of adventure sport.

2

Colder than Everest

The story of these early years is one of self-doubt and self-reliance, the excitement and ecstasy of every moment of fresh adventure and a chance for bravery.

— Fred Beckey, *Challenge of the North Cascades*

RESCUE REPORT FROM RON GREGG'S 1980 DENALI EXPEDITION.

NATIONAL PARK SERVICE
CASE INCIDENT RECORD

...ANIZATION CODE	2. ORGANIZATION (PARK) NAME		3. LOCATION CODE	4. CASE/INCIDENT NO.		
9 1 2 0	Mt. McKinley NP		0 5 3 0			4 7
...ATION OF INCIDENT	6. WHEN MO. DAY YR.	24 HOUR TIME	HRS. MIN.	7. DAY OF WEEK		
...ylor Spur, Mt. McKinley	0 4 0 6 8 0	2400		1		
...ENSE/INCIDENT CODE	9. NATURE OF INCIDENT	10. HOW REPORTED				
7 0 0 6 0 1	Frostbite: Mountaineering	Radio				

...PORTED BY / San Diego Calif. / PHONE / HOME / BUSINESS

...CEIVED BY OGER ROBINSON / 15. WHEN RECEIVED 4/11/80 / 16. TIME BROADCAST

...VESTIGATED BY OGER ROBINSON / 18. OFFICER/RANGER NO. 021 / 19. WHEN INVESTIGATED 4/11/80 TIME 140c / DISPOSITION

INVOLVED PERSONS	22.	23. ADDRESS	PHONE	24. SEX	25. RACE	26. AGE	27. DATE OF BIRTH
		San Diego, Calif.				26	

...TAILS OF INCIDENT

March 17, 1980, Ron Gregg and [ ] left Park Headquarters to ski to ...der Lake and the Muldrow Glacier. They planned to climb Pioneer Ridge and to ...e Taylor Spur for their approach onto the ridge.

April 4, they had reached the 10,500 foot level of the Muldrow Glacier, at the ...e of the Taylor Spur. On April 6, they began their ascent of Taylor Spur, ...volving steep, difficult ice climbing. This day they ascended 6 pitches, reaching ...a ridge crest of the spur at 12,500 feet at 2300 hours where a small ledge was ...pped in the ice and an open bivouac was made. The temperature this night was ...to 20° below zero with some wind.

...next day, April 7, [ ] noticed he had frozen both large toes. ...two moved their camp to a better place to stay over the ridge crest. They ...up a tent at this location. On April 8th and 9th they remained at this site, ...iting to see the seriousness of the frostbite. Once it was determined that the ...stbite was more serious than anticipated, the decision to descend was made.

April 10, after the 4th night at this elevation, descent was made back to the ...p site at 10,500 feet on the Muldrow Glacier. On the evening of the 10th, they ...the Marmot Mt. McKinley Expedition of three members, led by Bill Lokey, who ...nned to climb the Pioneer Ridge also.

...TITY	30. PROPERTY STOLEN OR DAMAGED	31. ESTIMATED VALUE	32. DATE	RECOVERED 33. VALUE

...PERTY CODE HIGHEST VALUE / 21. TOTAL / 34. TOTAL

...IGATED BY (Signature and Date) / APPROVED BY (Signature and Date)

NATIONAL PARK SERVICE
SUPPLEMENTARY CASE/INCIDENT RECORD

ORGANIZATION (PARK) NAME		CASE/INCIDENT NUMBER
Mount McKinley		4 7
LOCATION OF INCIDENT.		DATE OF INCIDENT MO. DA. YR.
		0 4 0 6 8 0

NATURE OF INCIDENT
Frostbite

COMPLAINANT'S NAME	COMPLAINANT'S ADDRESS

RESULTS OF INVESTIGATION

[ ] wished to be rescued and the Marmot Expedition carried a Radio Anchorage unit, so a call was planned for the next morning. On April 11 at 0845, John Scott placed a call to Radio Fairbanks stating that [ ] had frostbitten toes and needed evacuation. Their location of 10,500 feet and ½ mile east of Taylor Spur was given. In a later radio call Scott described [ ]'s frostbite as both big toes frozen and blistered and that one blister was oozing.

At 1200, 4/11/80, a Jet Ranger helicopter arrived from Fairbanks and at 1210 it departed for the mountain with ranger Dave Buchanan on board. The pick-up of [ ] was made at 1300 hours at the 10,500 foot level on the Muldrow Glacier. At 1355 the helicopter arrived back at McKinley Park airstrip. Ranger Roger Robinson interviewed [ ] for this report and at 1415 the helicopter departed with [ ] to Fairbanks Memorial Hospital.

Ron Gregg remained at 10,500 feet through a several day storm, then descended the Muldrow Glacier following wands left by the Marmot Expedition. On April 24, Ron returned back to Park Headquarters.

It appears in examination of [ ]'s foot protection that his supergaitors were inadequate, especially for an open bivouac on Mount McKinley in March.

...BMITTED BY (SIGNATURE AND DATE) Roger Robinson 6/22/80 / APPROVED BY (SIGNATURE AND DATE)

While nearly 10,000 feet shorter than the world's tallest mountain, the highest summit in North America is a fearsome beast. It was briefly named Mt. McKinley by westerners, but writers of modern history, and the USGS, have returned the mountain to its native, and arguably far more poetic name: Denali.

The mountain has a base circumference bigger than all of Colorado's Rocky Mountain National Park, and the heavily glaciated north face, known as the Wickersham Wall, is one of the world's largest uninterrupted mountain faces, with 14,000 vertical feet of relief.

Many mountains are higher than Denali (20,320 feet), but there may be no mountain that appears bigger from a distance. The base elevation is only 2,000 feet above sea level, giving the peak an 18,000-foot profile. The base of Everest, by comparison, sits at about 17,000 feet for a 12,000-foot profile – making Everest a vertical mile shorter than Denali in terms of visual, and climbable, relief.

Denali and the surrounding Alaska Range is an environment that park ranger Daryl Miller calls "some of the most challenging and committing terrain in the world." The summit is at 63 degrees latitude – nearly 2,500 miles farther north than Mt. Everest. The lowest recorded temperature on Denali is −100°F/−73°C, at 15,000 feet; Everest's record low of −76°F/−60°C was recorded on the summit. Doug Scott, the legendary Everest climber from Great Britain, famously said that the weather on Denali was the worst he'd ever experienced.

A booklet produced by Denali National Park, to alert interested climbers to the dangers of the peak, explains the harsh potential of Denali weather in no uncertain terms:

> In winter months, the jet stream, 100+ mph (160 km/h), will often descend over the mountain's upper flanks. Combine this wind with the naturally caused venturi effect that doubles wind velocity in such areas as Denali Pass and you will find one of the most hostile environments on this

planet. The combined effect of ferocious wind and extreme cold easily and routinely sends the windchill off the charts.

Ironically, it was Ron's career in nuclear physics that opened his eyes to the world's potential for full-throttle recreation. After receiving his doctorate from Caltech, Ron was hired to help invent and use a three-colored laser designed to measure the settlement of earthen dams. With aging dams all over the world in need of accurate monitoring, Ron found himself frequently traveling overseas. With an appreciation for natural places, and the energy of an unwalked dog, Ron would finish a project quickly and then stay in the area to explore. According to Ron's brother, Bob Gregg, it was on these trips, including projects in Africa, Asia and Europe, that Ron caught the travel bug and decided he wanted more from life than a prestigious career in science.

In 1979, Ron decided climbing Denali was more important than the company where he worked. He quit his job and directed all of his scientific thought and boundless energy into preparation for an expedition to one of the coldest mountains on earth.

Ron wasn't the kind of climber to be satisfied with following the path of least resistance to bag a trophy summit. Instead, he chose to attempt an unclimbed variation to Pioneer Ridge, a serpentine buttress of ice and rock bordering the massive Wickersham Wall. The name Pioneer Ridge is a bit misleading in that it was not the route used on the first ascent of the mountain. In fact, the ridge has proven to be a difficult and rarely climbed feature on the popular peak. The name comes from early explorations on the peak that attempted the ridge – most likely chosen because from a distance it is the peak's most obvious route to the summit.

To prepare for the trip, Ron's first stop was REI, the store with the widest selection of mountaineering boots. But Ron didn't just go shopping – he went researching. Armed with graph paper, a scale and a painfully critical mind, he sat down in the shoe section and asked to try on every boot in the store. The lightweight plastic

RANDY KING AND RON GREGG WEARING PROTOTYPE X-GAITERS
AT THE SUMMIT OF THE BROTHERS, OLYMPIC MOUNTAINS,
WASHINGTON.

double boots used today for high-altitude mountaineering were just a year away from entering the market, so the best possible options were all heavy, with a sturdy leather outer boot and an insulated bootie-like liner.

An easygoing young man named Randy King was working for REI at the time and helped Ron find the right boots. Randy recalls the memory of Ron's obsessive boot-shopping frenzy as if it happened yesterday. Ron took every boot apart, weighed the liners, the outers, all the different combinations possible, and took notes on everything. He had boots and liners spread out everywhere. Randy must have helped Ron find the right boot – in 1983, Ron would ask Randy to help him run his newly formed outdoor company.

To minimize the amount of fuel needed for the expedition, Ron and his partner committed to enjoy only one warm meal per week. Using their fuel only for melting snow, but not heating the water to a high enough temperature for cooking, allowed them to survive on one liter of fuel per week. In contrast, the fuel allowance for guided ascents of Denali is one cup of fuel per person per

X-GAITERS

Supergaiters for X-C Skiing, Hiking, Climbing, & Telemarking

THE WARMEST GAITERS MADE

COMFORTABLE, SLIP-PROOF TOP CLOSURE

TASLAN GORE-TEX®

REMOVABLE FOAM INSULATION

WIDE HOOK-AND-LOOP FRONT CLOSURE

DUAL LAYERS OF RUGGED WATERPROOF FABRIC

TOUGH, FIELD – REPLACEABLE SHOCK CORD AROUND WELT

THERE'S REALLY NO REASON FOR WET FEET OR COLD TOES

Outdoor Research
Seattle, WA

THE ORIGINAL X-GAITER ADVERTISEMENT, SHOWN WITH THE SKI SYSTEM RON GREGG USED ON HIS FATEFUL DENALI EXPEDITION.

day, or nearly four times Ron's daily fuel ration for the climb. Ron tested the effects of cold on different foods, finding that Havarti cheese, peanut butter, summer sausage and peanut M&Ms were still edible straight out of the freezer.

Ron's plan was to eschew the glacier flight used by most Denali climbers, and instead ski nearly a hundred miles from the highway near Wonder Lake before even beginning the climb. Without dog sled or airdrop support, Ron's approach would be considered exceptional even by today's most highly trained and well-equipped mountaineers. The vast majority of ascents in the Alaska Range, including those by elite modern alpinists on hard first ascents, start from a ski plane drop at the beginning of the steep terrain.

The long approach to Denali's north side complicated and increased the adventure factor immensely. Without a cell phone, satellite phone or even a two-way radio, Ron and his partner left the road near Wonder Lake looking at a 100-mile ski and an 18,000-foot climb.

In 1980, the mountain boots didn't work well in skis, and the ski boots didn't work well for climbing. So they chose to ski in wobbly but light cross-country boots and skis, and drag their mountain boots to the base of the climb on sleds – along with 45 days worth of food and supplies.

To protect their feet from the early-season Alaskan cold, in both ski and mountaineering footwear, the climbers designed gaiters that covered the upper part of their boots entirely but left the soles free to accommodate the ski bindings on the approach and crampons on the climb.

Once they reached the technical terrain, the same gaiters could be switched from ski boots to mountaineering boots. This gaiter style is called a supergaiter, and at the time, other supergaiters attached to the foot with a rubber band that was stretched over the boot. The trouble with the rubber band was that it inevitably slipped off the toe of the boot, and even when it stayed on properly the rubber did not provide much insulation. With temperatures on Denali in March potentially reaching −50°F or lower, insulation mattered. To allow the gaiter to be insulated all the way to the sole, Ron designed an attachment system using a wire or cord that tensioned around the welt between boot and sole and crossed under the boot for additional security.

The gaiters were one of many homemade or modified pieces of equipment they customized for the climb. Ron's sled was made of a pair of his sister's skis, and his backpack was entirely handmade, a boxy, zipper-accessed thing he called the Refrigerator. Ron's attention to durability was obsessive – the Refrigerator didn't blow out until 17 years later, on a ski run in the Yukon.

Inevitably, on such an expedition, teammates spend a lot of time together in the confines of a small tent. Tent time with a know-it-all can be both educational and irritating in the extreme. And Ron Gregg was the consummate know-it-all. He was infamous for knowing everything, even things he should know nothing about, and the fact that he was almost always right drove his friends and family mad. Years later, when Bob Gregg's children were curious about something, Bob would say, "Call Uncle Ron."

Once, Bob's son was preparing for a math test and was given one of those classic math questions with a certain number of chairs and a certain number of people, and the goal was to figure out how many different combinations of seated people there could be. When his son couldn't figure it out, they called Uncle Ron. Ron listened carefully and then asked, "Do you need combinations or permutations?"

Not knowing for certain, they opted for combinations, and Ron quickly gave them the answer. Bob, still startled at Ron's razor-sharp mind even after a lifetime together, asked, "How do you do that so quickly?"

"Well, any fool knows that." Ron replied, giving his usual caustic answer to why he knew the answer to a difficult question.

Another time, Bob gave his children a telescope for Christmas. They were trying it out and suddenly Drew, Bob's oldest son, said, "I see a planet and I think I can see moons."

"Moons?" Bob replied. "Let's call Uncle Ron."

"That's Jupiter," Ron replied, without hesitation, "and you're seeing Io, Europa, Ganymede and Callisto."

"How do you know which moons we're looking at?" Bob asked. A valid question, considering the planet has 63 of them.

"Well, those are the only ones that can be seen with a regular telescope."

"How do you know that?"

"Any fool knows that Galileo was arrested by the Catholic Church in 1633 for finding those moons and suggesting the orbit of the planets."

Another time, after a lifetime of his big brother getting the upper hand, Bob thought he'd finally came across a problem where he could win an intellectual triumph over his brother. True to the brainy tendencies of the Gregg family, Bob was managing a software company that provided data calibration for computers and military applications. Y2K was approaching and the topic was at the forefront of Bob's daily work. Not only was the millennium changing, but leap year needed a reset as well. A leap year occurs every four years, but every 100 years the leap year is skipped, and making it even more confusing, every 400 years the skipped leap year is skipped. So 2000 was indeed a leap year. Such are the idiosyncrasies of the Gregorian calendar, and Bob was sure he finally had a question Ron couldn't answer.

He called Ron and asked, "Will there be a leap year in 2000?"

"Of course."

"How do you know?"

"Well, any fool knows that you have a leap year every year that is divisible by four, but not by 100, except when it's divisible by 400."

Not only did Ron know, he had the simple equation in his mind that made the answer obvious to him.

"I give up," Bob replied.

There would be no shortage of interesting tent conversations, high-level problem solving and testing of intellect on an expedition with

Ron – especially one to the north side of Denali in early spring. For 18 days, the two climbers skied across the snow-covered tundra to reach Denali. At the base of the enormous north face, they left their skis behind, strapped on their crampons and began working their way up the technical part of the climb. The previously unclimbed terrain consisted of long stretches of moderate alpine ice broken by steep bands of granite. After a long day of climbing, they were unable to find a suitable spot to pitch their tent.

According to the National Park Service rescue report, the two endured an open bivouac, meaning they were benighted, without tent or shelter, at 12,500 feet with temperatures reaching −20°F and moderate winds to drive the chill even lower. During the technical climbing and open bivouac, Ron's partner suffered frostbite on his toes. They climbed higher to a place where they were able to pitch their tent. What happened after that may never be known, and Ron's partner's insistence on not telling his version of the story publicly has only fueled the fires of speculation as to what happened.

The most farfetched story suggests that the two had some kind of disagreement that resulted in the frostbite. Another story is that after they found a place to set up the tent and get warm, Ron soloed higher before returning to help his partner descend. According to the Park Service incident record, the two spent a couple of days at their high camp and didn't climb above 12,500 feet, but it is quite possible that the ranger reporting on the rescue never learned of Ron's solo. It is also possible that they just festered in their tent for a few days, recovering from a difficult night in the open and wondering whether they should continue climbing or descend.

Ron was known to be both a caring and competent partner and none of his adventure partners ever spoke ill of his decision-making, but he was also known for doing his own thing, sometimes wandering far from the team without explanation. It is quite possible that he soloed easier terrain above the camp – not on a hell-bent summit mission but just to experience a little more climbing before the inevitable retreat. Regardless of the details, the two were able to reverse their route and make it safely back to Muldrow Glacier. As luck would have it, on the glacier they met another team attempting Pioneer Ridge – and the second team had a radio. They called the National Park Service for a rescue.

In a moment of quintessential Ron Gregg, when his partner was airlifted out, Ron declined the helicopter ride, opting to ski back to the road by himself, taking nearly two weeks to remove the food caches they'd left behind, at a time when the grizzlies were just waking up, hungry from hibernation. It was a strong statement of staying as true as possible to his human-powered vision, and it allowed him to complete the expedition without leaving anything behind in the Alaskan wilderness.

The descent from any big mountain is a time when the mountaineer's tired mind tends to wander between both the climb that just happened and what life will bring upon returning to the civilized world. Ron was 32 years old, disenchanted with his career, and captivated by adventure. Skiing alone across the tundra for a hundred miles, after a climbing adventure in the deep-freeze world of the north side of Denali, completed an experience that inspired profound changes in Ron's life.

He never went back to the halls of science. The National Park Service rescue report reads: "It appears in examination of (Ron's partner's) foot protection that his supergaiters were inadequate, especially for an open bivouac on Mt. McKinley in March."

What caused the frostbite is largely irrelevant; the injury had cost the two friends their dream climb, and as a direct result of the expedition Ron started a company devoted to making outdoor equipment that is designed precisely for the environment where the equipment is used.

The company needed a name, and with a fundamental philosophy of using the experience of adventure as the driving force in designing the gear, he opted to name his new company after that experience – a quest that would outlive Ron himself and inspire one of the most apt brand names in history: Outdoor Research.

3

The Adrenaline Lab

Never had concentration made so much noise in my head. I was a simple shell of forces and movement ... My excitement was explosive as I screamed to release the fullness; I felt I belonged here.

—Mugs Stump, "Hunter's North Buttress Direct,"
American Alpine Journal, 1982

RON GREGG AND KAJ BUNE PRODUCT TESTING ON THE
BRABAZON GLACIER, WRANGELL-ST. ELIAS RANGE, YUKON.

Ron came back from Denali absolutely convinced that he could design better gear than anyone, and he was tired of being a physicist. After Denali he was somewhat interested in the post-doctorate research position that was still waiting for him at Caltech, but what he really wanted to do was run the Grand Canyon again, paddle more whitewater and go climbing.

An ongoing joke in his family, when Ron would rant about this or that lame piece of equipment, was "If you're so damn smart, why don't you make it yourself?" With the creation of Outdoor Research, Ron took his family's advice, but as is common in business, the final form was a bit different than the original inspiration. At first, Ron hoped to be a consultant for outdoor brands already in existence. While a decade later such work became a meal ticket for outdoor athletes to travel, climb, float, hike and ski, in 1981 nobody was going to hire an outside consultant to design gear. Knowing one thing for certain – that he didn't want to work for anyone else – Ron turned away from nuclear physics forever and poured his obsession with function and design into perfecting the X-Gaiter, a better-insulated version of the supergaiters he and his partner had used on Denali.

Eventually he had a design he felt would be worth selling and approached local backpack maker Dan McHale to help with production. Dan agreed to make the gaiter, and although Outdoor Research sold $50,000 worth of X-Gaiters the first year, Ron quickly realized that the market for such specialized equipment was incredibly small and that he needed a second product. His sister Laurie, with whom he had shared many adventures, had the idea to make a first aid kit with a soft cover for wilderness use. She had already made a version for herself, and it suited Ron's personal obsession with organization perfectly. He was quoted years later in *Outdoor Retailer* magazine as saying, "I'm one of the few people in the world making a living by being anal-compulsive. The high degree of organization in our medical, travel and various outdoor kits is a direct result of my personal urge to organize. The fact that our product designs are very 'clean' derives directly from my personal predilections."

REI placed the Outdoor Research first aid kit on the back cover of its 1982 catalog and the first order of 1,000 sold out immediately. The product gave the fledgling company a huge boost. Fifteen years later, Outdoor Research would offer 17 different versions of the original medical kit, targeted at different genres of outdoor sport. There was an Outdoor Research first aid kit for every application. With advice from his father, Ralph, who was a medical doctor, Ron crafted customized first aid kits for guides, mountaineers, backpackers, hikers, saltwater and whitewater enthusiasts, family camping, and adventure travel. Every detail of the kits was considered to the utmost.

In a not uncommon version of the old story of the innovator not reaping the rewards of his designs, the travel first aid kit was copied copiously and sold by companies far less specialized and with much more marketing horsepower than Outdoor Research had at the time. The copying of his products aggravated Ron to no end, but there was little he could do about it.

Both ironically and unfortunately, with the magnitude and frequency of Ron's adventures into wild places, he and his partners knew firsthand what contents should be in each specialized first aid kit. Ron's appetite for adventure travel, with *adventure* taking precedence over *travel*, led him to rack up a phenomenal amount of time in the wilderness. Over his 22 years at the helm of Outdoor Research, Ron left Seattle to spend between one and three months a year in what he called The Big Office, and he wasn't going to places on *Outside* magazine's top 100 lists. As his wife, Sharon, explained, "He wasn't really interested in the usual destinations. He would take out the map, put his finger on a blank spot and go there."

Over the nearly four years total Ron spent in the woods during

DR. OR HIMSELF, RON GREGG, PH.D.

his tenure at the helm of Outdoor Research, three of his partners were evacuated in helicopters, and there were the sprains, breaks, cuts and bruises that inevitably accompany great adventures if you spend enough time out there. Among his friends, the phrase "Ron-related injuries" was a common topic of conversation. Of all the Ron-related injuries, the most dramatic one also helped to inspire Outdoor Research's next product.

Ron's sister Laurie married a fellow adventurer named Dave Nicol, and the three of them together enjoyed kayaking in Glacier Bay, ski touring in Yosemite, rafting in Hells Canyon, sailing in the Caribbean and mountaineering in the Cascades. One winter, Ron and Dave decided to climb Mt. Rainier via Disappointment Cleaver, the most popular route to the summit. The peak receives 10,000 ascents during the summer months, but in the winter it's a much more serious challenge, and you can almost count on being the only climbers on the mountain.

After one unsuccessful attempt, they returned and made good progress despite a couple of feet of recent snow and camped at the base of the climb. The second day, they climbed through exhausting soft snow and camped again at 11,000 feet. On the third morning, they packed light for the summit and set off. With −15°F temperatures and 30 mph winds, the windchill was −46° and it very much felt like a winter ascent. Upon reaching the top of the Cleaver, a broken buttress of rock that cleaves the chaotic ice of upper Ingraham Glacier, they decided they'd had enough. Dave explained their decision to turn back simply: "Ron never was that much into summits."

On the way down, while they were traversing unroped off the bottom of the Cleaver formation, Dave's crampon caught on his gaiter and he tripped. Falling anywhere else on the route would have most likely been fine, but at that particular point he plunged over a 100-foot cliff and onto the steep and crevasse-riddled

Cowlitz Glacier. Ron was just out of sight around the corner, and when Dave didn't show up, he returned and found the tracks where Dave had slid over the edge.

It is easy to imagine the horror that must have been going through Ron's mind at the sight of his brother-in-law's out-of-control track disappearing over a cliff high on the slopes of Mt. Rainier. Ron traversed around the cliff and easily found Dave's track again in the soft snow, continuing along a trajectory onto Cowlitz Glacier. Ron plunged down the glacier, likely with little heed for his own safety, and after an hour and half of searching he eventually found Dave, alive, standing dazed near the edge of a large crevasse – 1800 feet below where he'd fallen.

With the short winter day giving Ron no time to go for help, and with their winter camping equipment out of reach at their high camp far above, they both wriggled into Ron's bivy sack. Dave had brought one as well, just in case something untoward happened on their summit day, but in the fall his pack had exploded. He'd also lost his gloves in the fall and his fingers were already frozen before their long winter bivouac even began.

Considering Dave had fallen over a hundred-foot cliff and then tumbled for a third of a mile down a steep glacier, his injuries were relatively minor – thanks to the deep snow that cushioned his fall – but his shoulder was smashed to the point where it would never work properly again and he would lose parts of all but one finger to frostbite. Walking out under his own power was not an option. In the morning, Ron left Dave tied in to keep him from wandering in delirium, and charged off the mountain to get help. It took Ron most of the day to navigate the crevassed glacier and descend another 4,000 feet. At the road, Ron found a ranger and explained the situation.

At the very moment Ron was talking to the ranger, an Army National Guard helicopter was flying over the mountain. Using an emergency channel, the ranger was able to contact the helicopter

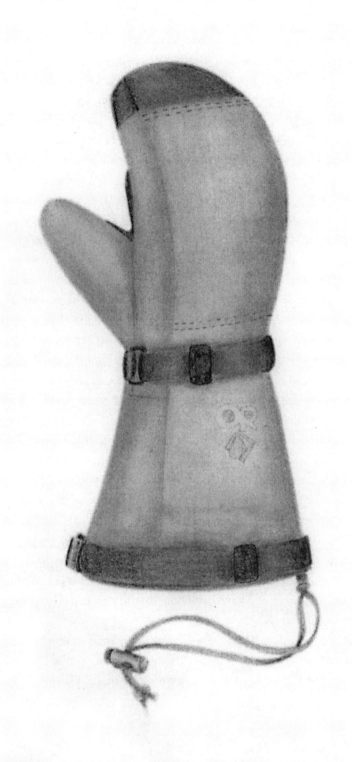

pilot, and the chopper changed course and plucked Dave from the side of Mt. Rainier within minutes after Ron reached the road. Had the helicopter not been in the area, Dave would likely have been forced to stay on the mountain for another night.

Dave told me this story twenty-five years after the incident, from his living room in south Seattle. He told the story without pointing blame or discussing regret, his frostbite-scarred hands resting comfortably in his lap, in a position of acceptance. Dave concluded his story of the fall by turning his gaze to the waters of the Pacific and said, "I don't know how well I'd have survived another night."

Despite all the Ron-related injuries, none of Ron's partners suggested he was a dangerous partner. In fact, they suggested quite the opposite. The ones I spoke with said he was smart, strong, concerned for his friends and made good decisions with few mistakes. Karl Kohagen, one of Outdoor Research's first reps, remembers forgetting his helmet for a day of whitewater kayaking with Ron. Ron insisted that Karl, the less experienced boater, wear his helmet. "I felt guilty and nervous all day," remembers Karl, "But that's just the kind of guy Ron was."

A critique of Dave's fall could easily point out that they should have been roped up on the Cleaver, but it is impossible to accurately judge a decision made in the mountains if you weren't there at the time. The soft snow surely made them both feel comfortable climbing unroped, and they most likely didn't anticipate the violent stumble that follows catching a crampon on a baggy gaiter. In some mountain terrain, tying into a rope only means that if one falls, the other will be pulled off as well. If Ron and Dave had both fallen, nobody would have been able to initiate a rescue and they both would most likely have perished.

After the incident, Ron vowed to make regular gaiters to complement the already successful X-Gaiter, but they would not be the loose-fitting, baggy ones everyone else made. Gaiters at the time were, as Karl Kohagen put it, "one-size-fits-nobody," with elastic bands at the ankle to pull in the extra fabric. Dave's fall inspired Ron to make the world's first sized gaiter, with a streamlined fit in three different sizes to keep the fabric out of the way and prevent a dangerous stumble. After making a few prototypes, with design suggestions from Randy King, Ron again found himself in the REI boot section, this time trying his new fitted gaiters on every boot in the store to make sure the sizing and cut were right for every boot on the market.

The new gaiter was, as Ron would put it, "an instant classic," and it needed a name. Karl remembers sitting in the car, waiting for an avalanche closure on Stevens Pass after a day of skiing, and pondering a name for the new gaiter. The most popular gaiters of the day were called Alligaiters, so Karl asked Ron, "What's bigger, badder, meaner and tougher than an alligator?"

"A crocodile." Ron answered.

To this day, the Crocodile is by far the most popular skiing and mountaineering gaiter in the world. In the late 80s they were the only game in town and everyone had a pair. Crocodiles were so prevalent that they became part of the unofficial uniform for outdoor adventure. From Talkeetna to Chamonix, groups of climbers could be seen standing around, every single one of them wearing a pair of the iconic red and black Crocodiles.

Carlos Buhler, the Himalayan veteran famous for the first ascents of the North Face of K2 and the East Face of Everest, as well as for his congenial manner while on expedition, observed that Crocodiles "really did establish a quality standard in this country" and that "they were the product that established Outdoor Research as a top-quality brand."

Years later Lacoste, with its crocodile logo, threatened to sue Outdoor Research for having a product named the Crocodile. Randy King explains Ron's reaction to the threat simply: "He basically gave them the finger." Having seen some of Ron's writing,

I can only imagine what his written variation of the finger must have been.

The success of Crocodiles fanned the flames of the Outdoor Research team. The company was growing quickly and their reputation for quality and function was no secret. Climbers on expeditions sponsored by competitors were known to smuggle their Outdoor Research gaiters up the mountain for summit day. Several different Outdoor Research employees from those days told me similar stories, and all of them smugly finished their story by saying, "And we got the summit shot."

By this point, Outdoor Research was indeed a team. Everyone played hard, worked hard and somehow contributed to the innovations. Outdoor Research had become the unrivaled king of outdoor accessories. According to Karl, "Everyone else was treating accessories as an afterthought."

The market was ripe for better handwear, but as usual it was an adventure, rather than any sort of market research, that provided the impetus to design a new glove. Again Mt. Rainier provided the harsh winter conditions and Ron's friends provided the critical near miss. Ron, Karl and Randy went on an overnight ski tour on the lower slopes of the mountain, each sporting different handwear. Karl wore form-fitting, insulated ski gloves, which were really warm and worked great – until they got sweaty and soaked at the end of the first day. On the second day, when the gloves were just as wet in the morning as they had been the night before, Karl knew he had a long day ahead of him and it was all he could do to keep his hands from freezing. With Karl working hard to keep his fingers, the incident ended without injury, but the need for a better system was obvious. Ron and Randy wore mittens, and were able to maintain warm fingers at the cost of dexterity. At the time, there were a couple of pieces of handwear intended for mountaineering, but they were either poorly designed, wore out quickly or were made in

Europe and had been marked up three times by the time they reached American climbers.

Back in Seattle, the team set to work creating a mountaineering mitten with a modular design that allowed the liner to be pulled out to dry. At about the same time, Carlos Buhler began working with Outdoor Research as a sort of design consultant. The relationship was one of the first of its kind, as the professional climber/ambassador concept didn't really take off until the early 90s. With a climbing resume a mile long, and a penchant for high-altitude mountaineering, Carlos was a perfect candidate to extend Outdoor Research's experiential design onto the world's highest peaks.

Carlos's girlfriend at the time made him a pair of shell mittens for Everest. They included a generous gauntlet with a wide swath of Velcro. When worn over Dachstein mitts, they provided the best high-altitude handwear available at the time. Carlos was quick to point out that exactly how much his gloves influenced the Outdoor Research designs is unknown – OR was combining all the best ideas from athletes like Carlos and business associates like Randy King and Karl Kohagen, so the final product, while overseen closely by Ron, was certainly a team effort.

For Outdoor Research's first glove design, Ron drew a seam pattern on his hand with the goal of creating a glove to fit the hand's natural curvature. He walked around the office for weeks with the slowly fading glove seams still inked on his hand. Both the glove and the mitten were designed around the modular ideal, a liner that could be removed to dry. After seeing how poorly gloves and mittens worked in the demanding conditions of the Pacific Northwest, the team was convinced that the layering approach used on the rest of the body needed to be extended to the hands.

Layering a glove is a simple idea but tricky to execute, and it was a rocky road for Outdoor Research products to go from the design phase to the retail shelf. Ron believed with conviction that each design needed to be thoroughly tested in the appropriate environment before the product should be sold, and that it was utterly unacceptable to use customers as gear testers – a trend that aggravated him to no end in the rapidly growing outdoor sector. In the early 90s, Ron wrote in the Outdoor Research catalog, "We try to subject each hat, mitt, gaiter, travel kit or first aid kit to all the uses and abuses that the consumer might. We try to see it through their eyes and thus make a product that really works. We seldom get it right the first time. Or often even the tenth time. But we get it right before we start selling it."

Climbing and skiing in prototype layered gloves revealed just how easily the liners pull out of the shells when you try to briefly take your hands out of the glove, so Ron added small Velcro strips to hold the fingers of the liners into the fingers of the glove. This way, the liners stayed put until the climber wanted to take the liner out to dry, eliminating frustrating and time-consuming finger fiddling. As with other Outdoor Research products at the time, experiential design was a recipe for success, and Karl recalls, with a voice like a proud parent, "We completely dominated handwear really quickly."

While Ron is known as the idea machine behind Outdoor Research, he would have been the first to point out that the other people in the company suggested ideas that would go on to influence successful products, but sometimes it took a virtual blow to the head for Ron to realize the merit of their ideas.

Karl and Randy had been trying to get Ron to produce a bivy sack – an ultralight shell that can be put over a sleeping bag on outings where a tent is deemed too heavy – but Ron was not convinced. Karl even had inside information from working as a rep for other outdoor companies that showed the demand for bivy sacks was adequate to make it worthwhile for Outdoor Research to get into the game. Still Ron was not convinced.

That summer, Ron, Karl and Randy hiked in to try one of the long, high-altitude rock climbs on the East Face of Mt. Whitney. The five-mile walk from the trailhead, with packs already heavy with climbing equipment, made the trip the ideal adventure for using bivy sacks rather than tents. After getting stormed off the face, the three climbers descended to their camp at Iceberg Lake, where they crawled into their bivy sacks and proceeded to get pounded by rain all night long. To understand what camping in a bivy sack that is not waterproof would feel like, imagine filling a garbage bag with cold water, climbing inside with your sleeping bag, and trying to go to sleep.

In the morning Karl turned to Ron, both of them about as dry as if they'd slept *in* the lake, and said, "Do you think we should make a bivy sack now?"

Ron replied, "What do you think I've been doing for the last nine hours."

Before they hiked out, Ron asked Karl and Randy to join him on the beach, where he drew the first Outdoor Research bivy sack design in the sand on the shores of Iceberg Lake.

4 The White Room

Panic, terror, suffocation – not even our lifejackets could save us there. Something to think about, I think, as I contemplate the imminent disaster, and meditate on possible alternatives to a sudden, sodden personal extinction.

—Edward Abbey, *Down the River*

KAYAKERS ON THE TOBY RIVER, BRITISH COLUMBIA.

Until recent times, the modern genres and sub-genres of outdoor adventure were called the same thing: *exploration*. There was little need to differentiate. The mountains, rivers, deserts and oceans presented more or less the same challenges and rewards. The tools and techniques were different, but the goal of going into any true wilderness, where few, if any, humans had ever gone, satisfied the need for adventure in an explorer's psyche.

Sport was a concept reserved for either traditional athletics, where the result was a clear winner and loser in a carefully controlled environment, or for the hunting of animals by people who didn't really need the meat for food. It wasn't until the prominent summits had been scaled, the mighty rivers run and the seas all sailed that the term *sport* became a common way describe adventure.

And even now, for many modern explorers, the transition from adventure to sport isn't a complete metamorphosis. Ron Gregg was one of those explorers who had little interest in becoming a specialist of one genre of adventure. For him, the differences between climbing on the flanks one of the world's great mountains and running one of the world's great rivers were immaterial. He must have realized that the specialization of adventure – and the resulting equipment innovations – was good for his business, but the Ron Gregg school of outdoor research was all-inclusive.

River running was an obvious adventure sport that could benefit from the functional innovations that Outdoor Research was becoming well known for, and designing quality boating gear fit the experiential design model that Ron so loved. He spent many months of his life on river trips, as likely to spend a Saturday afternoon playing on a wave on the Skykomish an hour outside Seattle as to run a classic like the Grand Canyon or organize an expedition to an obscure link-up in the Yukon.

In order to let the adventure be the driving force in design, Ron carried a graph-paper notebook everywhere he went. Even on an ultralight river trip where each person had a ten-pound weight limit for personal gear, Ron found space in his dry bag for his notebook so he could work on designs.

He obsessed over the details of gear like a man possessed. He once complained to Toyota about the design of their cup holders. He bought a microscope so he could study the details of the fibers in each material Outdoor Research used. He knew the stitch length of every fabric the company used. Then he went out on the river and watched how the fabrics and designs performed in the water, grit, sun and abuse of a river trip, and took copious notes on all of it.

Ron's obsession with details didn't stop at the gear. He carefully considered every element of an adventure as if he were sending a spaceship to the moon. "He lived (on expeditions) on peanut butter and bagels – individually wrapped." Remembers Sharon Gregg, laughing. "He'd buy five different bagel flavors and leave them sitting on the counter to see which ones molded last. Everything was an experiment for Ron."

When Ron would return to the Outdoor Research factory after a month or two on the river or in some exotic mountains, he would enter the office bursting with the intensity of the experience he had just had, and with a head and notebook full of ideas he wanted to implement. Ron's absences, and then whirlwind returns to the office, inspired great products, but they were hard on the team at Outdoor Research. Randy King liked to say, jokingly, "I could leave the office anytime I wanted, except when Ron was on a trip, or when Ron was home and I had to help implement all the ideas he came up with on his trip."

One of Ron's closest friends, and one of the few friends of his who never worked for Outdoor Research, was a happy-go-lucky boater and expert skier named Lance Young. For the better part of 30 years, Ron and Lance shared adventures at every opportunity. Ron could stay up all night. Lance could wake up before dawn.

They were the perfect road trip team. "With most people, planning a trip was this big complicated thing." Lance remembers, smiling fondly. "With Ron it was just one phone call: 'Do you want to go?' 'Sure.'"

When Ron would take off on a trip, as Joe Wadden, a long-time Outdoor Research employee explained, "The company would slow to a crawl." Sometimes that crawl was barely functional. Once, Ron left with Lance on a river trip to the South Fork of the Salmon just before payday, and with nobody at the office with the authority to sign paychecks and Ron 500 miles away getting ready to put in for a long river trip, mutiny was brewing.

"There's no way I'm going to miss this trip just to go sign checks," He said to Lance. Instead, he paid a premium price on an airline ticket so his girlfriend, Rebecca Wallick, could fly to Boise with the paperwork to give Randy the authority to sign paychecks. Ron met her at the airport and signed the papers. She got on the next flight back to Seattle and Ron went boating.

It's been said that Outdoor Research prospered because of Ron and in spite of Ron. His travels were hard on the OR team, but his travels were also where his best ideas were born. Something about the rhythm of life on the water allowed him to simultaneously indulge his insatiable fun hog as well as consider the details of design without the distractions of managing the factory. Randy remembers, with equal parts frustration and fondness, that "Ron would come back from these trips with all these ideas."

Of all Ron's adventurous hobbies and habits, he was probably most proficient, and perhaps happiest, in a kayak. So while few of his designs were specifically for kayaking, it was the environment where he could consider projects and details from the Zen perspective that comes with utter contentment.

"He'd be floating along singing Disney songs." Remembers Lance. Once at the campsite, Ron was the kind of guy who would be the last to go to bed and the first to wake up in the morning. He would scribble things in his notebook at all times of day and night. Campfire chatter would gravitate to Ron's intellect, with long conversations around topics like the relative impact of a nuclear blast at different distances from ground zero. On side trips from the river, Ron would go farther than anyone else wanted to go. Lance remembers one side trip in the Middle Fork of the Salmon on a layover day where Ron woke everyone up before dawn and dragged them on a jaunt that entailed 9,000 vertical feet of hiking in the Bighorn Crags before staggering back into camp well after dark.

Ron and Lance were notorious for showing up at a campsite four or five hours later than everyone else. The two friends couldn't resist a good wave, and they played on every ripple they could stick. This was in the days before low-volume "playboats," but the mesmerizing thrill of motionless speed while riding a bucking kayak on a gurgling hydraulic has little to do with the shape of your hull.

Ron became an icon in the outdoor adventure world because of his inventions and his commitment to his company, but his lesser-known adventures on the river reveal just how far he pushed the ideal of letting adventure design Outdoor Research products as well as Ron Gregg's life.

There was no environment where Ron's gear innovations and subsequent adventures were more outrageous than on the water. Once, he decided to paddle the South Fork of the Skykomish, at flood stage, alone. Like many of his solo missions, it wasn't that he really wanted to go solo, it was that he couldn't find anyone to go with him and he wanted the experience so badly that he went alone. He asked Lance and a couple of others if they were interested. "It was too big," remembers Lance. "Usually, I'd go on anything unless it was just loony."

Undeterred, Ron went anyway. To increase his chances of survival if he got sucked into a gnarly hole, he wore a scuba diver's buoyancy compensator vest with a CO_2 cartridge attached. If needed, he would pull a cord, the CO_2 would inflate the vest, and

OUTDOOR ADVENTURE À LA 1980s.

the added buoyancy would bring him to the surface – or at least that was the idea.

Part way through the run, he did get sucked into a nasty hole, in the Boulder Drop behind the picket fence, the toughest rapid on that stretch of river even at normal flow, and was forced to abandon his kayak. The powerful water pinned him below the surface, so he pulled his emergency cord. The vest inflated, but in a rare moment of poorly executed Ron Gregg theory, he had the vest on *under* his life jacket (or PFD in kayaker speak) so instead of inflating outward as it would have outside the confines of the PFD, it pressed inward and partially collapsed his lungs. One can only imagine Ron's terror as he tumbled in the whitewater, bubbles tap dancing on his eyeballs and the air pouring out of his lungs as his invention backfired terribly.

With equal doses of luck and strength he escaped the hole and staggered to a nearby road where he tried to hitchhike back to his car. Bloodied from close encounters with underwater rocks, and dressed in that slightly strange wetsuit-and-spray-skirt-look, he couldn't get a ride. So, adding insult to injury, he had to walk all the way back to his car.

Another time, Ron took a small oxygen tank and scuba face mask on a Grand Canyon trip and ran the biggest rapids looking like a very out of place Jacques Cousteau. He never tested the scuba face mask as he did with the buoyancy compensator, but he had it along during what turned into his biggest river epic. With mixed experience in the group, Ron, Lance Young and Karl Kohagen, the most experienced boaters, paddled kayaks, while Luke Gjurasic and Bob Straub paddled in rafts.

The team's troubles began at Chrystal, one of the more infamous of the canyon's big rapids, when Luke managed to pin the supply raft against a boulder. Luke jumped onto the boulder, and Ron, Lance and Karl ferried across and eddied out under the boulder to help. Despite their best efforts, the raft was being held in place by all the force of the Colorado River and it wouldn't budge.

They were able to pull a few things from the raft for spending the night, but their food supply had been washed off the stricken boat. As the sun set, the rest of the team paddled to shore, but Luke stayed on the rock so he could, theoretically, jump on board in case the river released the raft during the night. Every hour or so, someone would yell to Luke to make sure he was okay.

At some point in the wee hours of the morning, Glen Canyon Dam increased its release flow, and the water rose over the rock where Luke waited. The water washed around his ankles, then knees, and he stood, bracing against the current in the center of one of the most enormous Grand Canyon rapids, in the middle of the night, with the water rising around him. Realizing he was doomed to swim the rapid in the middle of the night, Luke decided to preempt the inevitable, grabbed a couple of things from the raft to give him extra flotation and jumped into the rapid. In full darkness, he swam the rest of Crystal.

Sometime later, the boys on the shore yelled at Luke but there was no answer. When the light of dawn finally wriggled into the canyon depths, the six eyes on the shore, straining into the disappearing gloom, were met with a terrifying sight. Lance remembers, two decades later, with intensity in his voice as if it happened yesterday: "We looked out in the morning and Luke was gone."

Ron and Lance, fearing the worst, jumped into their kayaks and paddled downstream looking in every eddy and behind every rock. Within 15 minutes, they saw the figure of a man lying on a rock. "We yelled, and threw rocks near him but he didn't move," remembers Lance. "We thought he was dead."

But Luke was merely napping soundly in the sun after a sleepless and horrifying night. With no food and not much camping gear, the team continued down the river. A river trip with all the comforts of home became a scavenger hunt for food and equipment. Instead of playing on the waves, they prowled eddies looking for flotsam. By evening they'd found a single can of fruit cocktail. Dinner that night was divvied out a single piece of fruit at a time.

As they went farther down the canyon, the pleasures of floating the most famous river run in the world became a hunger-driven quest for food. "Every day was like a special delivery," says Lance.

Continuing down the river with growling stomachs, the team salvaged bits and pieces of their food and equipment stuck on logs, washed up on beaches and swirling in eddies. They would intermittently stop in the sun to dry their soggy stores. Karl laughs at the memory: "We spread the wet stuff out on flat rocks to dry. It felt like we were a bunch of Indians drying our food. We'd eat whatever we found, no matter how wet and muddy it was."

Near the end of the trip, while navigating Lava Falls, Bob paddled the supply raft directly into the biggest hole in the rapid. In a split second, the 16-foot boat was sticking upright out of the hole. Bob was flipped out of the raft and disappeared downriver into the maelstrom. Lance and Ron paddled downstream, looking for Luke, fearing the worst, until Bob's shrill whistle broke the tension. They found him circulating in an eddy, pissed off and relieved. The second mishap ended uneventfully, but afterwards Ron pulled out a small bottle of whiskey that had somehow made it though the entire adventure. Karl remembers, laughing, "It must have been in his boat the whole time!"

While Ron was busy surviving river epics, and testing gear to the limits of his abilities, Outdoor Research was taking on a life of its own. In 1989, the company was listed in *Inc.* magazine as one of the fastest-growing companies in the country, but the world of human-powered adventure was changing in ways that would eventually test the limits of Ron's ability to engage in obsessive product testing and simultaneously manage a complicated business.

By the mid-90s, adventure sport had moved far from the murky pools of the lunatic fringe and was beginning to feel the pull of the mainstream current. In 1993, Atomic launched its Fat Boy ski, making deep-powder skiing possible for average skiers. In 1994, Lynn Hill free climbed the Nose of El Capitan in Yosemite in a day, one of most transformational feats in the history of climbing. In 1995, snowboarding held its first World Cup tour in seven countries and the inaugural summer X-Games were held in Rhode Island. Low-volume kayaks were turning boating into a playful, hip sport for young people. Hiking shoes were lightweight and comfortable. Waterproof/breathable fabric was actually waterproof and breathable. Mountain sport suddenly became a lot more fun.

Riding the wave of healthy growth, Outdoor Research in 1995 burst the seams of their downtown Seattle location and moved into a seven-storey industrial office at 2203 1st Avenue, just south of the city, on the edge of Puget Sound. The building would serve as both a launch pad and an anchor for the next era of Outdoor Research, a time that would reveal both the opportunity and pitfalls that have accompanied the globalization and normalization of adventure sport.

5

When It's Not About the Fun

Our society encourages an achievement orientation, but is less effective in encouraging the effort that leads to the achievement.

—Arno Ilgner, *The Rock Warrior's Way*

WORKING AT THE GORE SEAM TAPING MACHINE AT THE OUTDOOR RESEARCH FACTORY IN SEATTLE, WASHINGTON.

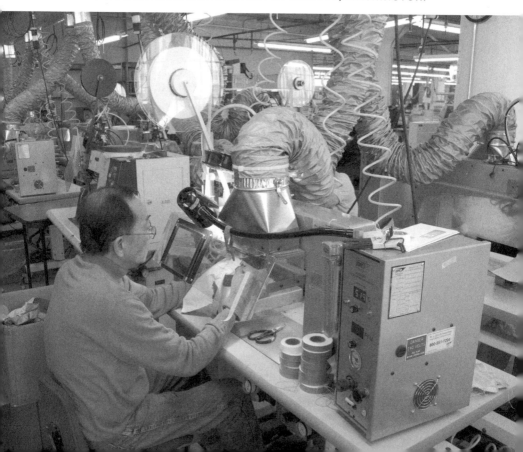

The Outdoor Research global headquarters stands in the heart of southern Seattle, or SoDo as the area is affectionately known. SoDo is steeped in a hip industrial ambiance unique to the west coast of America. A hundred yards to the south of Outdoor Research stands the Starbucks building. To the west, a sea of shipping containers and 50-ton container cranes stretch for hundreds of yards along the Port of Seattle, the sixth-busiest in America. The hundred-year-old Filson factory is visible to the east of Outdoor Research, and bakeries, cafes, specialized industry and get-anything-you-want bars line the street to the north towards downtown Seattle.

Viewed from the outside, the Outdoor Research building defies modern categorization. It's the kind of place where Willy Wonka would make chocolate. The lattice-reinforced windows on some floors speak of a different time, before cubicles, mirrored commercial glass windows and offshore manufacturing. A glass top floor suggests a modern corporate facility and gives the place a mysterious blend of history and cutting edge. Upon closer look, a humble sign with the Outdoor Research brand hangs on the corner – dwarfed by a mural-sized coffee advertisement on the building next door. Inside, the Outdoor Research headquarters is a striking juxtaposition of an old-school American industrial atmosphere blended into a new-school adventure-sports cultural center.

On the ground floor of the building, the Outdoor Research Factory Store, selling everything from the most recent OR products to technical climbing equipment and guidebooks, gives the visitor open doors into the heart of the company. The elevator is decorated with a 300-degree panorama of the North Cascades' Mt. Triumph loaded with late-winter snows, and the corporate offices on the top floor are a modern marriage of glass and wood, with an open floor plan enabling nearly every desk to have a window view. Comfortable conference rooms with heavy wooden tables are designed around all the tools of efficient modern communication.

Just a few feet away from the digital projectors and CAD workstations of the office floor, the Outdoor Research factory floors are a glimpse into an America of the sort our grandparents told us about, one of the only places in the United States where technical products are still manufactured in their entirety under one roof. Eighty sewing machines are lined up in rows, with dozens of operators peacefully working through stages of assembly-line-style product construction. The very sound of the factory tells a story: the hum of sewing machines; the heavy, irregular thump of die presses cutting patterns; the quiet, happy chatter of workers whose movements are so ingrained that their hands can execute fine motor skills while their minds and discussions drift somewhere else. With a backdrop of earthquake-cracked windows framing the Seattle skyline, the entire scene is a timeless snapshot of American entrepreneurial spirit.

At high tide, seawater floods the bottom of the elevator shaft and the faint smell of the ocean lingers in the air. In the basement, a climbing wall has been constructed, complete with a couple of cracks just the right size for training rock climbers, and a slackline – a climber's tightrope. In one corner sits a stack of well-used kayaks, in another a gas grill.

Many of the workers have been employed on the Outdoor Research factory floor for a decade or more. Some got their job on a recommendation from their parents, who had got a job through a recommendation from their parents before them. Dalisay Detorres, the day shift supervisor, has been working for Outdoor Research since she emigrated from the Philippines in 1989. "One-third of my life I've spent here," she says, looking around at the factory proudly.

"They are always looking out for the comfort of the workers," says Dalisay. "That's why we are happy here. If we are not happy here, we will not stay. We have 15-, 17-, 18-year employees. The management, they understand us. If they didn't, personally I will not stay. I will go."

The workers are a mix of people from all over the world: China, Vietnam, Thailand, Cambodia, Greece, Burma, Korea, the Philippines, Hong Kong. Most of these workers got the job through friends or family connections. Dalisay laughed as she explained: "My sister-in-law needed a job, then my sister needed a job. Now they are all happy working here."

The sewing-machine operators are paid by the piece, not by the hour, so efficiency is important to their earnings. Dalisay views her role in the factory as helping the workers to be comfortable and to maximize their productivity. She says, "I'm here to teach them how to make sewing easier."

The easy relationship between the management and the workers makes the overall goal more clearly understood by everyone. Dalisay concludes our conversation by saying, "If we are the instrument to make Outdoor Research grow, I am happy to help because then we all have jobs."

Today's Outdoor Research factory owes its productive hum to two drastically separate factors: Ron Gregg's almost parental management style, and the world's appetite for war. The first was both a blessing and curse for the company. For Ron, every person who worked at the factory, as well as every product produced, was a child of his. He could no more easily fire a seamstress or cut an item from OR's product line than most people could get rid of a beloved pet or leave a child at a foster home.

Even when the rest of the apparel industry was paddling offshore as fast as they could, Ron Gregg, with an almost suicidal commitment, kept Outdoor Research's manufacturing in Seattle. In the 90s, when most of OR's competitors were outsourcing their entire product line, 90 per cent of OR's line was still made at the Outdoor Research factory, and with labor in Seattle costing 12 to 15 times more than labor in China, Ron's loyalty to his factory was taking a toll on the bottom line.

By this point, offshore manufacturing was an accepted reality of modern business, and it was an impressive feat indeed that the company had remained competitive while refusing to source overseas. Part of the brand's tenacity was its reputation among loyal buyers and core users, and part of it was the proprietary techniques the Outdoor Research factory offered. One of these was the seam-taping technique for creating truly waterproof gloves and mittens of Gore-Tex.

Dan Cauthorn is an experienced climber who was working for the W.L. Gore factory at the time and facilitated the development of the seam-taping technology at the Outdoor Research factory. He explained that while the idea seems simple at first glance, the reality is much more difficult and that OR was far ahead of anyone else in taking the Gore-Tex technology into new applications. Thanks to Ron's aggressive integration of Gore-Tex into Outdoor Research products, he already had an intimate working relationship with W.L. Gore. "Ron really challenged our perspectives at the time," explains Dan. "He was an early advocate of the whole Gore-Tex technology. He really understood the technology and how it works with human comfort and physiology."

Gore was already using what they called a "bootie drive" machine, which had an arm with a taping roller on the end, to seal the inside seams of the Gore-Tex liners used in running shoes and hiking boots. The tool was too big to work on gloves and the thumbs of mittens, though, so Outdoor Research worked with Gore to create a seam-taping machine that would fit inside the smallest fingers of the smallest gloves.

Outdoor Research was the only company in the world with Gore licensing and technology for taping the seams of Gore-Tex handwear. W.L. Gore, a company whose success hinges on careful licensing of its technologies, also allowed Outdoor Research to modify its seam-taping machines to produce the world's first seam-taped Gore-Tex gloves. Even today, only a few places in the world can seam-tape inside the fingers of Gore-Tex gloves. Most companies making Gore-Tex gloves buy pre-made liners from W.L. Gore and insert them into their glove designs. While these liners have gotten better and better, they still don't fit into the glove as perfectly as the Outdoor Research gloves built with Gore-Tex liners sized to the exact specifications of the rest of the glove.

Producing the finest gloves in the world on US soil made Outdoor Research the obvious choice for any highly demanding application where gloves are necessary. On the wall in one corner of the modern Outdoor Research factory hang finished samples of the products made there. A dozen different gloves, all of them grey, camouflage or olive colored, are designed for combat. These gloves will never touch a cork 720, an ice axe, a pillow drop, a gondola or a ski pole handle. These gloves will instead keep US soldiers' fingers functional during long hours in uncomfortable posts in unimaginable places.

Climbing guides across the United States train Special Forces in technical climbing skills, so information is passed from the most experienced climbing culture to the elite tactical culture. A Special Forces commando once said to their guide before a training session: "Don't teach us the watered-down, extra-safe version of climbing you teach your regular clients – teach us what *you* do up there. It's not like Uncle Sam is going to sue you if one of us gets killed."

This means the commandos want to know how to lead and make decisions themselves. They want to know how to best use marginal anchors if necessary and how to quickly transition between different kinds of technical terrain. They want to know which gear the guides use on expeditions to the wildest mountains. This means guides can pull out all the stops of institutional guiding to give military groups as many climbing skills as possible in a short amount of time. While most climbing students spend years learning the basics before doing their first lead, the Special Forces sometimes lead a climb on day one.

Learning to lead your first day of climbing is not necessarily fun, but for military climbing applications it is not about fun. The military will most likely use their climbing skills and equipment in places where nobody has ever climbed before, on poor quality rock that no climber would ever choose to climb, and for a purpose that is the polar opposite of recreation. They are exceptional learners. The elite soldiers can learn the basics of rock climbing in a couple of hours, and then tie in to the sharp end (what climbers call the leader's end of the rope) and cast off into the vertical.

The military groups often buy gear based on recommendations from the mountain guides they train with, so with Outdoor Research gloves already the accepted gold standard in the guiding world in the 90s, it is no surprise that the military started phoning OR looking for the most waterproof and durable gloves money can buy. The US military has a policy that requires clothing used by its troops to be American made, so Ron Gregg's stubborn refusal to move OR's manufacturing offshore meant that his factory was still fully operational when the military began contacting Outdoor Research in search of better gloves.

Military-issue cold-weather gear was antiquated, most of it straight out of the Korean War, so in 1996 the Marine Corps decided it was time to examine and retool their entire line of winter gear. One of Outdoor Research's customer service reps, Tim Davis, began to receive inquiries from the Marines, and he grew curious about the possibility of developing a more formal line of business with them. First, the Marines decided to procure a small number of the Pro Mod glove and the Mutant Modular Mitt to test.

The Marines like the gloves and decided to make the Outdooor Research gloves and mittens the official Marine Corps handwear. The Marines placed a massive order accompanied by a hefty contract. "Ron didn't read the contract," remembers Tim. "And it had a clause in it saying that if we were late on delivery, we could be charged for the entire value of the contract. We delivered on time."

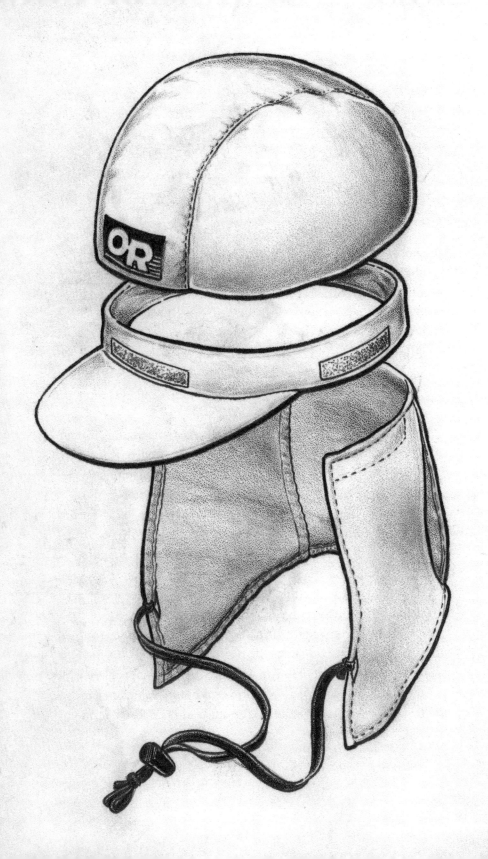

For the next eight years, Tim managed the military business for Outdoor Research. With inroads made with the Marines, OR also caught the attention of the Coast Guard, who eventually included three Outdoor Research products, the Windstopper Gripper glove, the Windstopper balaclava and the Power Stretch balaclava, in the official US Coast Guard Safety Manual as required cold-weather safety equipment.

Still, the products used by the military were exactly the same gloves used by climbers and skiers, and some of the features, like the flammable nature of the gloves, was still a weak point for military applications. To take the relationship to the next level, Tim decided to apply for a SBIR – a Small Business Innovation Research grant from the federal government's Small Business Administration Office of Technology. The agency website explains that it "ensures that the nation's small, high-tech, innovative businesses are a significant part of the federal government's research and development efforts."

The $50,000 grant gave Outdoor Research the funding needed to do basic research into what soldiers really needed. Ron was of course happy with the new aspect of the business, but he was reluctant to change the product for military applications.

Tim, who had been in the military years before, had a serious problem with military applications of the gloves that were designed for mountaineering. He felt that the fingers were too thick to fit within the trigger guard with enough clearance between glove and trigger. He told Ron he thought a soldier might accidentally fire the weapon while wearing the gloves.

"Bullshit!" replied Ron in his typical know-everything manner, "The Marines wouldn't buy them if they didn't work."

Ron had a point, but Tim was sure there was a problem with the gloves for military use. To prove his point, he bought a realistic rubber gun, brought it into the office and had Ron put his finger on the trigger while wearing the gloves. "It fit his finger like a fat man's wedding ring," remembers Tim, laughing.

But Ron still didn't buy it, so Tim decided only a live-fire exercise would convince him. They met at a firing range and Ron, to Tim's surprise, showed up with his own gun, a Colt .44. Ron put on the gloves, grabbed the gun, fully loaded, and started walking up to the firing line. "It was terrifying. I took the gun away from him and emptied all but one bullet."

Tim gave the gun back to Ron, who proceeded to take a shot. The recoil flipped the pistol out of Ron's grip and it proceeded to spin out of control around his heavily gloved finger. Tim explains the tense moment simply: "The gun was spinning around his finger like a gunfighter in an old Western." If Ron had fired the gun fully loaded, and had been using an automatic weapon instead of a revolver, he might have sprayed bullets all over the place.

Tim remembers that Ron just said, "Well, that fuckin' sucks."

It was a pivotal point for the Outdoor Research team. From then on, according to Tim, Ron Gregg listened a lot more carefully to what the rest of the team had to offer. Over time, the SBIR grant helped Outdoor Research to produce a set of four gloves that were designed to accommodate a soldier's fire-retardant, durability, color and function requirements in temperatures ranging from −40°F to +40°F. The four-glove system became a standard issue item for Special Forces, and OR's reputation for exceptional quality and American manufacturing spread through the military. Eventually, Outdoor Research was hired to build light assault jackets for the Delta Force and became the preferred provider of cold-weather handwear and gaiters for the Special Forces, the Marines and the Coast Guard.

6 It's Not About the Money

As he counted the frenzy grew on him, and when his task was over, and the old darkwood table was all yellow with gold pieces lying in stacks of ten, he was wild in the joy of his terrible lust.

— W.H.H. Murray, *The Story that the Keg Told Me*

RON GREGG ON A SIDE TRIP IN THE GRAND CANYON, ARIZONA.

At the other end of the spectrum from serious military work, the young, hip adventure cultures noticed Outdoor Research products thanks to the designs coming out of the Seattle factory. The Mt. Baker mitt had grown popular for snowboarding, another outdoor sport requiring especially sturdy and storm-worthy gloves and mittens, so it wasn't long before Burton, one of the corporate godfathers of snowboarding, caught wind of Outdoor Research's reputation and capabilities. By the mid-90s, the outdoor industry was at a size where mergers, acquisitions, hostile takeovers and all the trappings of big business were becoming common and potentially profitable. On a few occasions, Outdoor Research fielded and turned down buyout offers. Randy King, who was a minority owner of Outdoor Research by this point, handled those showing serious interest. When Burton offered to buy Outdoor Research for an eight-figure sum, Randy and Ron decided the time was right to sell.

Outdoor Research's following among mountain sport aficionados – plus a highly capable sewing factory on US soil, complete with proprietary technology and a partnership with W.L. Gore – made the company an appealing gem for Burton's already sizeable crown.

The Burton team visited Seattle, Ron wined and dined them at a fancy waterfront restaurant, lawyers crafted an agreement, and Ron and Randy prepared to become millionaires. For Ron, the concept of wealth held no significance. Here was a man who paid himself a salary of $90,000 a year even when his company was bringing in $12-million in annual revenue, drove the same beat-up, fiberglass-patched and jury-rigged Dodge Dart for most of his life, and only used his company's success selfishly to foot the bill for exotic "gear testing" expeditions. Contemplating life as a multimillionaire must have been an odd feeling. For Randy, on the other hand, a golden parachute out of Ron's manic world of on-again off-again micromanagement sounded very good indeed.

For the final meeting to close the deal, Ron booked a flight to Vermont to sign the papers. We can only imagine what was going through his head as he boarded the plane to go sign his name a few times and make enough money to spend the rest of his life playing on waves, sailing the oceans and climbing mountains. He got off the plane to make a connection at Chicago, but instead of connecting to Burlington he boarded the next plane back to Seattle. Ron called his brother, Bob, in the middle of the night after returning from Chicago. Bob remembers Ron saying simply, "I didn't do it." and then hanging up.

"That was a strange call," remembers Bob, the consummate businessman who has been in on the sale of 20 different companies over the years and successfully conducts his affairs with a strong conviction that everything is for sale at the right price. The Gregg brothers didn't talk about it much afterwards and Bob is still puzzled as to why Ron changed his mind. "That was very uncharacteristic of Ron. You didn't second-guess Ron – let alone Ron second-guess Ron."

Everyone around Ron at the time has a slightly different idea as to why he didn't make the sale. Sales manager Ted Steudel explained his theory clearly: "I don't think he could have sold the company to anyone, and he never, ever could have worked for anyone. If he had walked away with a wad of cash, he would have lost his friends and his purpose. I think he realized while going out there that 'whatever Burton would pay, it's worth more than that to me.' He was living his dream."

Randy King remembers Ron explaining it simply: "If I sold the company, who would I hang out with?"

Sharon Gregg, in whom Ron may have confided more than anyone else at the time, recalls several conversations about the decision and that he was uncomfortable with what would happen to all the people who worked in the factory and the office if he were to sell.

Her perspective matches Bob's prediction of what would have happened to the company in the long run if Ron hadn't died. "I think it would have gone the same direction it has today," explains Bob. "I think we were coming to a crossroads, and Ron would have realized he needed a broader product line and more capital to make it happen, but he wouldn't have partnered with anybody."

Bob also speculates that the pressure to go offshore "would have driven him to sell." This matches Sharon's perspective that it was the human factor that prevented Ron from signing the papers with Burton. If the factory work had been forced offshore, there would have been far fewer people close to him whose lives would have been affected by a change of ownership, and selling would have been easy.

Of everyone involved, Randy King took the decision hardest. He had already decided that if the sale didn't go through he would move on in life. When Ron returned without closing the deal, Randy resigned. "I was a millionaire on paper for six weeks," remembers Randy, laughing quietly.

The late 90s was a watershed era for Outdoor Research as well as the rest of the industry. Some of the qualities that had made OR a success in the marketplace of the 1980s began to hobble the company. Simultaneously, the basic business model was undergoing fundamental changes that required nearly every enterprise to retool significantly.

Back in 1981, when Ron founded Outdoor Research, most outdoor equipment innovators were not in the game to make money. In fact, for guys like Ron Gregg, that was part of the appeal of the industry. It was *all* about function. Ron designed things because *he* wanted the products for *his* next adventure. If enough other people liked doing the same kind of adventures, then selling the product could support a way of life for him and those closest to him. If buyers didn't want the product, according to his philosophy, they just didn't know what was good for them.

Ron became a successful businessman in his era precisely because he had no interest in being a businessman. In the 1996 Outdoor Research catalog, he wrote about his business learning curve:

> Being a scientist rather than a businessman, I had only the vaguest idea what it took to grow a company when I founded OR back in 1981. I had, in fact, negative total knowledge about business – which is to say that much of the little that I thought I knew about business was wrong and had to be corrected before I reached a state of mere ignorance.

He didn't succeed because he read market trends or even cared about them. He succeeded because he got into the business of making adventure more fun at a time when many young people were no longer satisfied with traditional sports and recreation. He succeeded because he maintained a dogmatic obsession with function – both the functioning of his business in providing security for its employees and the intended function of his products.

By the late 90s, game-changing innovations were harder to come by and the outdoor adventure market had matured. The fringe sports Ron loved, if not yet entirely mainstream, had become cool. Rock climbing was repeatedly voted as the sexiest sport and the number of Americans who recreate in the snow in one year was greater than the populations of Washington and Colorado combined.

In an interview in *Outdoor Retailer* magazine, Ron explained the approach that had, until then, worked so well for him:

> My lack of interest in fashion and my total involvement with function are directly responsible for our function-oriented product line. I like to work hard, to play hard in the outdoors, to have a lot of fun with both, to be highly irreverent,

to joke in the middle of serious meetings, to take our tasks seriously but not to take myself too seriously. These things show up the people we attract to Outdoor Research and the casual, highly interactive way we go about our business.

Ultimately, 90 per cent of Ron's philosophy was met with success, but the remaining 10 per cent – his utter lack of respect for fashion, his inability to retire aging products, his in-your-face-to-day-gone-tomorrow management style – began to take a toll on Outdoor Research. He was quoted in the *Seattle Times* in 1996 as saying, "Our basic success is not because we made products people wanted, but because OR makes products that perform in ways people didn't think they could."

Function *and* fashion were possible, and by the turn of the century much of the money spent on outdoor recreation annually was going to companies that offered healthy servings of both. Ron's commitment to being unfashionable was proving a hard sell to the new, normalized face of the outdoor industry. He once wrote in a mid-90s Outdoor Research catalog:

> Truth be known, there is a fifth (after innovation, versatility, durability and value), implicit guiding light in our design process. It illuminates a path that leads straight away from what is usually referred to as Style. We try hard NOT to design anything that will be in style for a while. Our products have an appearance that derives directly from the functional requirements. They do not follow any current fashion trends and don't have a "look" that will be in style this year and out again the next. Our Spandura pants will still look as unstylish in five years as they do now – but will work great and wear like iron! A Hat For All Season will still be Elmer-Fuddish in 10 years – but will still keep your noggin warm at 20 below! I would be extremely pleased if each of our products went out of style as fast as a Swiss Army Knife."

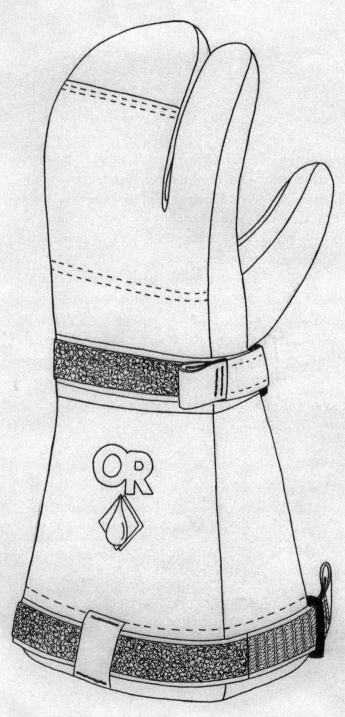

Mutant Mod. Mitt
CW 1-97

Karl Kohagen describes Ron's inspiration to enter the clothing market: "For a trip to Aconcagua, Ron reverse-engineered his favorite pants – Sears polyester jeans – and sewed himself a pair of pants made out of Spandura."

He took them to Aconcagua, where he climbed solo, without support from porters or mules and with no information except where the mountain was located. Ron would almost never look at guidebooks or research a route. For him, figuring it out as he went along was more than half the fun. Upon returning to Seattle, he had little good to say about Aconcagua's loose, toilet-paper-dotted slopes, but he was sold on the pants. Karl continues, "He came back raving about the soft-shell concept – and went on to render these pants that were completely unmarketable."

Ron was not alone in abhorring fashion, but along the dorky/chic continuum, everything we wear is a form of style, and even in the rough, functional worlds of mountaineering and skiing there is still a culture of fashion. Carlos Buhler recalls, with much mirth, the evolution of the mountaineering "uniform." In the early 70s, Carlos was introduced to climbing through what he calls "the gospel of Paul Petzoldt" at the legendary National Outdoor Leadership School in Wyoming, where the uniform was whatever could be bought at Army Surplus. From there they modified whatever was needed to make it work in the mountain environment. Carlos recalls, "We'd take the lower part of one sweater and sew the upper part of another sweater onto it." This created a sweater long enough to stay tucked in at the point where the pack belt or climbing rope tied around the waist.

A short time later, Carlos befriended a group of Spanish climbers and spent enough time in Europe to acquire a fondness for their mountaineering uniform – but he didn't give up his Army Surplus without a bit of a tussle. He remembers being confronted, in a friendly way, about his strong convictions in the gospel of Paul Petzoldt. "I was less experienced and they were very nice.

There was more than one way to skin a cat, and I didn't realize that."

The Europeans at the time were all wearing knickers and long socks and Carlos recalls buying a pair of wool knickers in Milan as somewhat of a milestone in his life as a mountaineer. Knickers prevented the dangerous scenario of catching a crampon on a pant leg, but knickers did nothing to keep the snow out of your boots. "Getting ahold of gaiters that worked was a challenge," says Carlos, "but they were a part of our uniform – they fit well with the knickers."

From this perspective, we all have a "uniform," whether we like to admit it or not. For Ron Gregg, sandals, a pair of jeans, a muscle shirt and a can of Pepsi was the uniform. For the telemark skiers of the 80s, the uniform was an Andean knit hat with earflaps, a dirty anorak, bib overalls with brightly colored knee patches, Vuarnet cat's eye sunglasses and Outdoor Research Crocodile gaiters. For snowboarders of the new millennium, the uniform includes baggy pants, plaid jackets and helmets shaped like those worn by WWII soldiers. All of these uniforms were at least partly inspired by rebellion against another style, but in the end they are still the uniform.

The function-over-fashion attitude is essential to making equipment work well in the wildest conditions. For commercial fishers, firefighters, soldiers, astronauts and others, function is the only thing that matters. But as wild as the mountains can be, the outdoor industry began to integrate urban fashion into technical products, and stylish clothing and accessories that also worked well began to enter the market. Still, Ron stubbornly refused to change.

Eric Cleaveland, a sales rep who worked with Outdoor Research for 22 years and has 37 years of experience in the industry, explained how there were several distinctly different factors besides

Ron Greg's personal vendetta against fashion that were conspiring against Outdoor Research.

One was an internal effort to upgrade to a modern, computerized business model that backfired catastrophically. To better handle the issues of inventory and all the other details of modern business, Outdoor Research invested in a huge computer program to manage the entire running of the company, including design, inventory, shipping, billing, manufacturing, payables, receivables and just about everything else. As it turned out, the conversion to the new program did not go smoothly and it almost destroyed Outdoor Research. For nearly three months Outdoor Research essentially did not function. All aspects of the company effectively got shut down due to glitches in implementing the new program. "It brought OR to their knees," said Eric. "The tolerance for (outdoor) companies operating poorly had come and gone. It was not a good time for the company to stub its toe."

Another factor was that many of the big buyers of specialty products had already begun to manufacture the same products under their own brands. REI, Cabelas and EMS, for example, all used to sell other companies' products exclusively, but when off-shore manufacturing and copying good designs became so easy, these companies began making products under their own name, charging less for them and making a bigger profit margin. This big-brand manufacturing made the retail floor of some of Outdoor Research's biggest buyers, once a haven of high-volume sales for the company, a far more difficult place to dominate.

At the same time, Chinese manufacturing techniques and standards had reached a quality threshold that could compete in the outdoor marketplace, so many competitors were able to offer lower prices on technical products while Outdoor Research, in order to pay wages to onshore workers, was raising prices on products that were quickly becoming yesterday's news.

Ron's stubbornness and resistance to change was the final

issue. There was an old joke at OR: "There is no such thing as a bad SKU" – meaning Ron felt that every Outdoor Research product was good and it didn't matter whether it sold or not. Eric recalls, years later with disbelief still in his voice, "Even in the face of the most compelling sales data, Ron wouldn't change his mind."

As a result of Ron viewing products as having value even if they didn't sell, new products were added to the Outdoor Research line without cutting the old ones. This inability to retire outdated and unpopular products created an internal inventory and efficiency nightmare as well as tarnishing the company's once impeccable reputation.

Eric explained that another element of Ron's management style was beginning to cause problems: he never went out and hired the best talent he could find, but instead promoted from within the company. This approach worked well at times and gave the company its legendary familial atmosphere, but the promotion-from-within philosophy sometimes put people in positions where they were not entirely prepared to perform.

As almost the final straw, Eric remembers buyers mentioning the growing popularity of competitors' products, and Ron replying, "If someone is stupid enough to buy that other brand's products, we don't want them as customers anyway."

The customer-is-wrong approach was hardly a way to move forward in business, so even with the factory's unique capabilities, stable military contracts and loyal customers around the globe, revenue began to decline and Outdoor Research entered the new millennium on its heels.

7

Perceptions of Risk

We spend our lives trying to evade death and its myriad of black mysterious faces, but unless we kick and shout back and fulfill ourselves wholeheartedly during our precious short time, death will stalk us until our days turn to mere condemnation.

— Jonathan Waterman, *In the Shadow of Denali*

OUTDOOR RESEARCH AMBASSADOR TOM MURPHY IN THE NORTH CASCADES, WASHINGTON.

According to the Outdoor Industry Association, by the early years of the 21st century three out of four Americans were participating in some form of active outdoor recreation (ranging from activities as benign as car camping to as extreme as BASE jumping) and in the process spending $730-billion a year and supporting nearly seven million jobs.

The ski industry has been a big part of the recreation economy for a long time, but back in Ron Gregg's heyday of the late 80s and early 90s, people were getting bored with tight turns and tighter pants. At the same time, snowboarding entered the mainstream and saved the game. The refreshing snow-sport concept of floating through just about any snow conditions – without decades of oversight by ski instructors to hamper creativity, and with an irreverent fashion and attitude borrowed from skateboarding – gave snowboarding an irresistible appeal.

The advantages of flotation provided by the wide board were painfully obvious, so ski companies jumped on the bandwagon to make fatter skis and looser pants, and sponsor bad-boy free skiers. For a while, the animosity between skiers and snowboarders was legendary. Snowboarding was lame because the snowboard was a hopeless tool in the backcountry, and skiing was lame because many skiers were more concerned with how they looked skiing than about how much fun they were having. Both sides forgot that, one board or two, everyone was doing pretty much the same thing.

Telemark skiing stayed clear of the fray, largely because until the 90s with the invention of modern alpine touring bindings, the telemark system was arguably the best way to access the backcountry. Telemark boots at the time were comfortable and warm and bindings were simple but durable cable or three-pin designs. The alpine touring bindings by comparison were heavy, didn't release when you wanted them to – resulting in injuries – and then released when you didn't want them to – resulting in frustrating and terrifying wipeouts. Snowboards were used on difficult descents in the backcountry, but overall the snowboard was a cumbersome tool in the backcountry.

Considering Ron Gregg's infatuation with all things backcountry, it is no surprise that he was drawn to telemark skiing, but his self-taught approach to everything proved more difficult with skiing. With mountaineering, you can slow down, consider the consequences of a mistake, and work through difficulties at your own pace. In kayaking, the technique is subtle and time-consuming to learn, but unless you drown, you get spit out at the bottom of every rapid you drop into and the only real way to learn is by spending time in the water – which Ron did to the tune of a month or two each year.

Learning to telemark ski without instruction, however, is a different kind of critter. Ron refused to listen to ski instruction of any kind, explaining in no uncertain terms that he wanted to learn on his own, and his ski partners all tell similar stories. His technique for both telemark skiing and dancing was known as the "gorilla technique" for his characteristic style of using force and enthusiasm rather than delicate finesse. Ron enjoyed both dancing and skiing immensely, but as soon as the ski conditions became difficult he would fall over on nearly every turn and the dancing is for another story.

"There is no mathematical way to figure out how to telemark," explains Sharon Gregg, a ski instructor and witness to many of Ron's ski epics as both wife and friend. "It was hard for him, but he was getting it figured out."

Ron's skiing was, by all accounts, a sight to behold. He was legendary for going on big ski tours, struggling to manage the conditions, falling on every turn, swearing at the top of his lungs with every fall, and then skiing up to the group as if everything were just as it should be without showing a hint of frustration.

On the south face of Mt. Superior in the Wasatch he fell on

every turn, swearing like a sailor, all the way down the entire 3,000-foot face. Located directly across from the Snowbird resort, the South Face of Superior is one of the most coveted and visible backcountry ski lines in North America. Not a single skier at Snowbird that day could have missed Ron's descent.

In the Cascades, he would be tree skiing out of sight of his group, but his swearing made his whereabouts obvious, so the rest of the group knew where he was, laughing at the spectacle of someone swearing so loudly and still having so much fun.

Perhaps Ron's biggest ski adventure was on a trip to a little-known corner of the Wrangell–St. Elias range in Canada's Yukon Territory in 1996. The expedition was a boondoggle inspired by the Outdoor Research design team of Bill Hartlieb, Carl Skoog and Kaj Bune. Kaj had been systematically working his way through the least-explored parts of the range, so when Bill suggested they get Outdoor Research to pay for it, Kaj put together a proposal for Ron, including marketing and design goals.

Brabazon Glacier fills a cirque surrounded by what were mostly unclimbed summits. It was the perfect place for the design team to carry on with Ron's school of outdoor research. Kaj remembers taking the proposal to Ron, him looking it over quickly and then saying, "Let's do it."

Kaj was thrilled. Then Ron added, "But one thing: I get to go."

"We hadn't thought of that," remembers Kaj. By then, Ron's reputation on adventures was legendary. He was notorious for going off and doing his own thing for hours at a time, and the stories of Ron-related injuries didn't help.

Karl Kohagen stopped Kaj in the hall before the trip and said, "You don't want to be on an expedition with Ron. He's totally unpredictable."

"I can handle it." replied Kaj.

With Ron's hard-man demeanor and legendary adventure style, Karl and Bill quickly decided they didn't want to share a tent with Ron. Kaj should tent with Ron. Kaj remembers their tent was made out of different fabrics so they could study how the condensation formed on each one. Ron scribbled their observations in his notebook, and this led to the final decision as to what fabric would be best for a new bivy sack design. As it turned out, Ron was a great travel partner. Kaj explained that he'd had nothing to worry about: "Ron was thoughtful, a team player, and was very well behaved. I was a little disappointed, actually."

They skied and climbed for three weeks, and near the end of the trip they skied back to the flattest part of the glacier, where the ski plane had dropped them off. After they picked their way through some crevasses, the glacier opened up into a perfect ski run and they unroped to enjoy an unencumbered descent.

In typical Ron style, he was wearing the same homemade backpack, known as the Refrigerator, that he had made for Denali in 1980. He fell immediately, and his waist belt broke, making his already awkward pack even more unruly. Kaj remembers, "The place was like a cathedral, and Ron was swearing so loud I felt as if I was with someone who was swearing in church. It was painful."

The Outdoor Research design team returned from the Yukon with renewed enthusiasm for their company and its direction. With Kaj and Carl both being crack photographers, the catalog that year demonstrated in no uncertain terms how the team of Outdoor Research did their own research, photography and adventure, and the trip ushered in a new era in the company's approach to business.

While self-confident and dogmatic to a fault, Ron was also about as smart as they come. He realized Outdoor Research stood no chance of competing in the long run with companies that were able to manufacture quality products overseas. Sharon explained the course of events that led to Ron's reluctant acceptance of offshore manufacturing. While he certainly was proud of his plant,

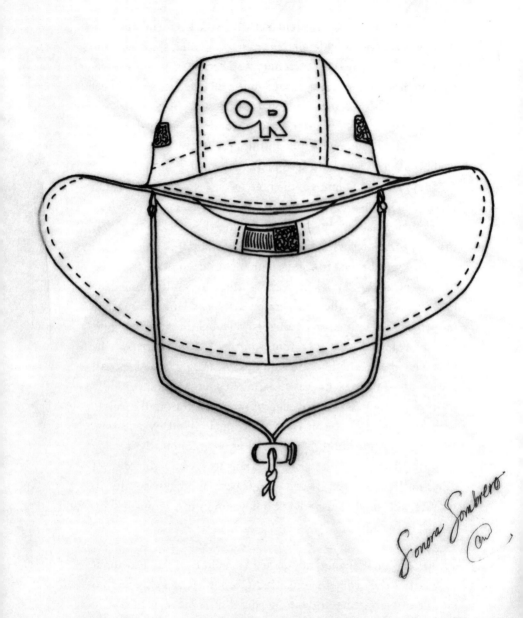

Sonora Sombrero
ⓒ

he was primarily concerned about conditions in the factories in China, and didn't want Outdoor Research products to be made in a place that subjected its employees to unacceptable working conditions. So he bought a plane ticket to China. While there, he decided that perhaps the manufacturing relationship between the western world and China would be the very thing that would elevate the Chinese to a healthier lifestyle. Explained Sharon: "Ultimately he thought (outsourcing) would help the Chinese people and at the same time help keep the US factory going. After his visit to China he said 'How will we ever help them change policy if their people are still poor?'"

Outdoor Research began outsourcing 10 per cent of production to Chinese factories. Product design had been Ron Gregg's domain and he was loath to let it go, but as he got older – be it natural maturity, surprising realizations inspired by out-of-control firearms, or simply a growing respect for the contributions of others – Ron began letting some design decisions go to talented people in the company like his Yukon partners Kaj Bune and Bill Hartlieb. He was slowly accepting that a good team was even more powerful than the smartest man could ever be.

However, even with Ron relinquishing some of his grip on design and manufacturing, his once industry-leading company was now playing catch-up in a difficult race. Outdoor Research's bottom line was shrinking every year. Big companies could quickly copy everyone else's best ideas; superior products were often trampled by the big players' marketing might; and breakthrough innovations are often in the form of nimble, innovative business models that provide the most desirable products on time and at the right price. Adventure was big business, and outdoor companies that did better business, well, did better.

The Outdoor Research catalog had always included a short introduction, always written by Ron, and by 2002 his writing revealed undertones of desperation, as if he were trying one last time to convince the world that fashionable brands were short on function. Ron wrote:

> Why should you buy OR products? Because I'm a Famous Climber? Well, I'm not, so that won't fly. Because OR is a really cool company? We are – or we like to think – but that's not a valid reason either. Because every outdoor product is made right here in Seattle? Nope, there's plenty of crappy stuff made in the good old USA. Because our products look great? Okay, lookin' great isn't our strong suit, and it's not much of a reason anyway!
>
> No, I don't want you to buy our products because of who I am, how cool OR is, where our stuff is made or how great it looks. I want you to buy OR gear because it really works. I've never been motivated to design gear that was particularly stylish or sexy-looking. But I'm fanatical about trying to design products that are as functional as possible."

Ron Gregg was a unique risk-taker in both business and pleasure. He presented a tough-guy image to the world with his prickly writing and intolerance for weaker minds, but everyone who knew him noticed that he had a feather-soft spot in his heart for people. He was willing to run rivers at flood stage by himself, but everyone he went on trips with talked about how he was the most careful explorer out there, always watching over the entire team to make sure everyone was doing well.

A BASE jumper (the sport of jumping off objects with a parachute) once explained that all jumpers begin the sport with two jars: a luck jar and an experience jar. In the beginning, the luck jar is full and the experience jar is empty, but with every jump, you take one unit out of the luck jar and put it into the experience jar. After a while, your luck jar is empty and the experience jar is the only thing keeping you alive.

By the new millennium, Ron Gregg's metaphorical experience

jar was full but his luck jar was quite empty. He had survived epics in the mountains, on the rivers and in business – sometimes thanks to his judgment and other times thanks to pure luck. By all accounts, Ron did not generally seek out the highest-risk elements of adventure sports, preferring fun and exploration over danger. For decades, his approach worked. Then, in March of 2003, he joined a group of friends for a backcountry ski trip to Kokanee Glacier Provincial Park in British Columbia. While skiing through Grizzly Bowl, Ron and two others skied ahead of the rest of the group. A large avalanche swept over them, burying all three. Two skiers, including Ron, were killed. Ron was 55 years old.

The year of Ron's death was a particularly lethal avalanche season in British Columbia. A total of 19 people were killed in slides in the province that winter, including one of the most tragic accidents in North American mountain sport history when seven teenagers were killed and many others buried by a massive avalanche on the most popular ski trail in Rogers Pass.

Ron and the other skiers had been aware of the dangerous snow conditions, but to a mountaineer such information is not necessarily a reason to cancel a trip. Danger is always out there, and any experienced backcountry skier knows that just because snow stability is poor doesn't mean you can't ski safely; and even when snow stability is good, avalanches can still occur.

Later, the survivors of the avalanche, all experienced backcountry skiers, explained to some of Ron's friends that before the accident they had all come to a mutual agreement to ski there, and that even in hindsight they couldn't really point to a dramatic mistake in their decision-making. In the end, critiquing a man's final choice is a fool's game anyway. Ron chose to spend as much of his life in the wilderness as he could manage, and skiing was just another vehicle to get there. It could have happened in a car, in the water or on a rope, but the snow is where Ron Gregg took his last breath.

Bob Gregg had this to say to the media the day after the accident: "We have been waiting for this call, you might say, for 20-plus years. And as sad as it is – and it only happened yesterday – the immediate thoughts that went through our minds were thank God it wasn't a car accident, thank God it wasn't a silly accident, or cancer or something like that. He did truly die as he lived, enjoying the outdoors."

8 The Adventure Portfolio

A critical aspect of creating a centered environment is to consciously choose as friends and associates those people who are committed, inspirational and powerfully active.
— Thomas F. Crum, *The Magic of Conflict*

WINSLOW PASSEY CLIMBING ON THE SOUTH FACE OF THE GRAND TETON, WYOMING.

At Ron's memorial, friends from high school and college commented that they had expected Ron to win a Nobel Prize, and were somewhat surprised by his off the beaten path in life. The next day, the Outdoor Research team and Ron's brother, Bob, got together at the OR office and tried to get a grip on what had just happened as well as what might happen to the company. Everyone had red eyes and there was more than one mighty hangover.

Joe Wadden explained the atmosphere in the room: "It was a strange feeling – we all felt like Ron was coming into the room any minute. We were all sort of just sitting there. We knew things had to happen, but they seemed meaningless."

Eric Cleaveland remembers, "We were there to consider every option, but ending OR and liquidating the company was never an option. We talked a lot about how Ron would have wanted the business to be handled."

Ron had willed his estate to his family, so suddenly Bob Gregg and his two sisters, Laurie and Lana, were left with the decision of what to do with their brother's company. Ron's siblings knew what they didn't want to do with Outdoor Research: they didn't want to take over leadership of the company, but neither did they want to sell their life's project to the highest bidder without considering what would happen to the company after the sale. Instead, they decided to look for a buyer who seemed most likely to move forward with the company intact.

At that point, Bob took over as interim leader, spending 60 hours a week at the Outdoor Research factory. Ted Steudel, a highly capable, sensitive and steadfast OR sales manager, stepped up to the difficult task of showing potential buyers around the factory and sharing the possibilities with Ron's family – while simultaneously hitting the sales telephones hard enough to keep the company afloat.

Ted had been hired after interviewing for the job from a dockside phone booth while wearing a spray skirt during a kayak trip around the outer coast of Vancouver Island in 1994. With his experience in the company and incomparable people skills, there was perhaps nobody better suited than Ted for finding the next owner of Outdoor Research. He explained that there were three elements to OR that needed to stay together to keep the company in its original form: the factory, the products and the people.

"There were sharks circling immediately." Eric Cleaveland remembers. "Some were ambulance chasers and they were immediately dismissed. Others were real possibilities."

"I walked the suits around the factory," remembers Ted. "The potential buyers all said 'I want the product but not the factory' or 'I want the factory but not the product or the people.'"

Then a man named Dan Nordstrom called and made an appointment for a tour. "He was the first guy who seemed to want the whole package," recalls Ted. "The stars aligned somehow. I could tell walking through the factory that he connected with people."

Tim Davis remembers, "We got to see a lot of folks walk through, and we could see pretty quickly that Dan was going to add a lot to the company."

Joe Wadden explained the reaction in the Outdoor Research offices at hearing of Dan's interest in OR: "It was fantastic news – complete acquisition with no corporate oversight."

A few Outdoor Research staff, curious to the point of sleeplessness about the destiny of their company, did an online search of Dan Nordstrom. When they found a photo of a handsome guy crawling across a log over a river with skis strapped to his back, the company breathed a communal sigh of relief.

Dan was already well in love with the world of adventure. Like many mountaineers of his generation, he had firsthand experience with Outdoor Research products and had owned the first X-Gaiters and the Mutant Modular Mitt. He also was cut from the cloth of gear modifiers, with numerous experiences customizing gear in the field with his trusty Speedy Stitcher awl.

In the 80s, Dan was already an accomplished ski mountaineer. In 1987 he was part of the team that first did the Thunder High Route ski traverse from Rainy Pass to Eldorado Peak in the North Cascades, unrepeated to this day. His partner on the trip, Lowell Skoog, wrote a story of the trip that was published in *Climbing* magazine. By the time Dan walked through the doors of Outdoor Research, he had done first ascents of alpine and rock climbs and served as president of the Access Fund, a non-profit dedicated to preserving access to climbing areas, during which time he received an appreciation award from the Southeastern Climbers Coalition for his work in preserving climbing access in the region.

When Dan Nordstrom quit his job with his family's department store company a week before his 40th birthday, he didn't really have a grand plan to get into the outdoor industry – he just wanted out of the publicly owned company world forever. Between riding his bike 20 hours a week and going skiing and climbing, Dan tried to figure out a new career. He was interested in acquiring an already established small business but wasn't content with just anything. He wanted something that was both intellectually interesting and financially promising.

After a winter of discontent, getting in his wife's way at home and looking at companies for sale that were either "interesting but financially tragic, or economically good but painfully boring," Dan took a trip to Canada to go skiing at Island Lake Lodge and discuss a new business idea with the legendary skier Scot Schmidt. After six straight weeks of epic snowfall, rising temperatures led to rain and heinous avalanche conditions, causing them to bail on the trip in the parking lot before even getting started.

Back in Seattle, Dan checked in with some of the people helping him shop for business opportunities. As fate would have it, one of his contacts was Jet Wales, who worked with the same firm that was handling Ron Gregg's estate. Dan had missed the news of Ron's death because he had been in British Columbia during the very same avalanche cycle that killed Ron. When Jet told Dan that Outdoor Research was for sale, he realized that the company might be exactly what he'd been looking for. Dan made an appointment to tour the plant that same Wednesday afternoon.

After the tour, Dan called two friends who knew the industry and asked them a single question: "Where does OR stand in the eyes of the industry at this point?"

They both had more or less the same answer: that while Outdoor Research had fallen in terms of market share, people fundamentally liked the company and were rooting for it. "That was the litmus test," explains Dan, "the economics weren't as important – I wanted to know what people thought of the brand."

Ron's brother, Bob, worked out the details to make the sale happen. From what Dan could tell, Ron's family was more concerned with giving the company a chance to continue, and keep the people who worked there employed, than with maximizing the revenue generated by the sale, so rather than wait for the highest bidder, they sold to the guy they felt would give the company a chance. "What (Ron's family) did was rare and profound," says Dan. "Other people were interested and the family could have waited and made more money, but they found a way to sell it to me."

On Saturday Dan signed a letter of intent to buy Outdoor Research. With high-caliber skills as a rock climber, ski mountaineer, mixed climber and ice climber, Dan stepped into the leadership of the company as if he were coming home. His method of taking over was, by all accounts, visionary. "He brought sensitivity to a difficult situation and handled it masterfully," explained Eric. "He treated people the way they should have been treated from the beginning."

First he took several weeks to just hang out at the factory and learn what the company was about before making any changes at all. Then he set about changing only the things that were causing problems, while leaving the company's strong elements intact.

This allowed Outdoor Research to move forward almost seamlessly while Dan executed the dramatic changes that were needed to enable the company to compete with global players in the modern outdoor market.

Before his death, Ron had just designed a new line of products, but instead of going ahead with production of the new designs, Dan shelved the new line, cut all the underperforming older products and hit the next sales cycle with a much-thinned Outdoor Research line. The sales reps were thrilled. It was exactly what they'd wanted Ron Gregg to do for years. Then he began putting together a team of the most experienced and energetic designers, marketing gurus and sales managers he could find.

He promoted some employees immediately, moving people like Joe Wadden into more responsible positions. Dan explained, "Ron was gone several months a year and the place still ran. There was lots of talent already in the company."

Outdoor Research had been affectionately know as "The Farm" because everyone who worked there grew up in the company. As Tim Davis put it, "Being home grown is a great recipe for a company too, but Dan brought in some new people who had really wonderful things to offer."

Eric explained that Outdoor Research was famous for not paying well, so when Dan started hiring it was a major change. "He started bringing in the best people he could find and paying the going rate. Things started happening. It was dynamic. People were empowered. And it was all because of Dan."

Having had his finger on the pulse of the industry for three decades by then, Eric Cleaveland watched the reaction in the trade to the new leader of Outdoor Research: "People went 'Oh, a Nordstrom! This should be interesting!' But anyone who took the

DAN CROSSES A LOG WEARING HIS X-GAITERS ON THE THUNDER TRAVERSE IN 1987.

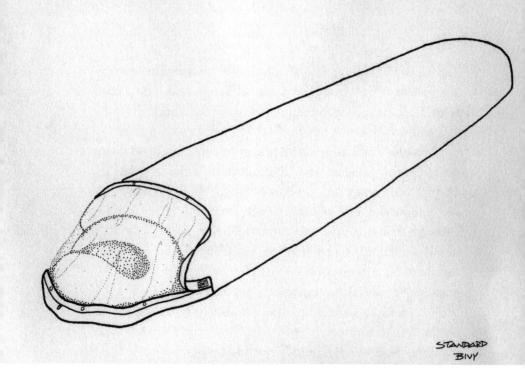

STANDARD
BIVY

time to see what Dan's CV consisted of would see he was as big of a dirtbag as the rest of us – and he could make good decisions. He had a compelling story to tell. He came in and said 'I'm going to make OR a better company, but not a different company.'"

One of the pivotal points in the new trajectory of Outdoor Research was when Kaj Bune, who had left the company a few years before, came back on board. Kaj had left because "Ron wanted the company to be like a family and he was the father. I already had a family; I wanted a career."

Kaj is a highly respected Renaissance man of the outdoor industry who has worked at a professional standard in design, photography, corporate, retail sales and journalism. His return to Outdoor Research sent ripples through the close circle of the outdoor industry. The message was clear: if Kaj Bune would go back to OR to work under Dan Nordstrom, then good things must be afoot in Ron Gregg's old factory.

With a redesign of the product line a matter of survival, Kaj suggested hiring Clark Campbell, a guru with experience in hands-on design as well as sourcing the manufacture of snowboarding and other outdoor clothing. For the rest of 2003 the retailers had had sympathy for the brand, and their goodwill kept the company afloat, but by the end of the year the message was clear. As Clark put it, "I got there and it was a short honeymoon. The retailers said 'We're not ordering as much this year, and if you can't come up with some new products, you can expect an even smaller order next year.'"

Clark's first job was herculean: redesign the entire product line for a well-established brand on an incredibly tight deadline; move most of the manufacturing to China to take advantage of cost savings and the most up-to-date manufacturing methods like laser cutting, laminated seams and external seam tape that were out of the question for the Seattle factory; do it without sacrificing the quality in any of the iconic products that are the brand's bread and butter; and do it all without creating such a hole in the Seattle factory's production that the workers lose their jobs.

The challenge was almost more than Clark could contemplate. When he first realized the task ahead of him he said to himself, "Oh my God, I've made the biggest mistake of my life."

Well aware of the challenge, Dan asked Clark if it was even possible. Clark replied, "I can get this done if I don't have to waste time explaining it to anyone."

Dan gave him the freedom to make it happen. Between January and July, Clark retooled the entire Outdoor Research line, cut the product categories of medical and travel completely, and introduced a skeleton line of apparel. To make sure the new products would give buyers a bit of renewed confidence in the brand, he contacted Gore and asked them to suggest their hottest new technology. It was the first of several times Clark would use his connections to move Outdoor Research forward.

Next, Clark traveled to China to find the right factory for production. He had two goals: convince the big factories to do business with Outdoor Research, and make sure the quality was at least as good as what the company was already making in Seattle. While meeting with a factory representative in Hong Kong, Clark realized it was not going to be the right relationship. He recalls, "I was telling them more about how to do it than they were telling me how they were going to do it – that's not good."

Going home and starting over was not an option, but you can't just walk up to a big factory in China and knock on the door. Without any other options, though, that's exactly what Clark did. He headed to China with a factory in mind, but knowing it wouldn't work without help, he called a friend at Nike and said, "I'm going to be on a boat tomorrow and I need an introduction."

When Clark arrived at the factory, he spoke with the guard at the gate. The guard checked with management and came back with bad news. "They had never heard of me and wouldn't let me in, and my driver had already dropped me off and was gone."

A short time later, the call came in that explained his situation and made the introduction. In the meeting that followed, Clark made a bold guarantee. He said, "I promise that in three years, we'll become one of your largest customers."

The factory began making Outdoor Research products, but a short time later the Chinese company operating the plant reached a point where it was growing so quickly that they decided Outdoor Research was not a big enough account. In an attempt to salvage the relationship, Clark and Dan visited China, and as Clark explains, that was a tipping point: "Dan's really good with people, and with his family name and what he represents to the retail industry we took something that could have been a disaster to our apparel business at that point and turned it around. Now we're one of their largest customers."

Not only had Clark been true to his promise of becoming one

of their biggest customers, Outdoor Research had helped the Chinese factory develop new capabilities. The plant in Seattle was instrumental in making the relationship purr. While most designers would show up at a Chinese manufacturer with a tech-pack full of drawings and specs, Clark would show up with a well-made sample that showed exactly how they wanted a product to go together.

Clark explained fondly the assets the Outdoor Research plant brings to overseas manufacturing: "We have some really good people in the factory in Seattle. Thong Nguyen is the best pattern maker I've ever seen. He can take a rough sketch and come back with a pretty darn good-fitting pair of pants." Thong's father had been a tailor in Vietnam, and he also received advanced design training in Seattle. Jerry Gundersen was another asset in the factory who had already worked with Ron on advanced concepts like torso venting and articulated fit and had vast experience turning the trickiest design concepts into reality.

In the office, Outdoor Research had settled into the new atmosphere of the company without the mighty presence of Ron Gregg. While Clark was on a mission to retool the product line, the veteran Outdoor Research crew were simultaneously facing increased responsibility and enjoying heightened freedom in their jobs. "Even though the name on the building still said OR," remembers Candice Springstead, marketing director at the time, "it was a totally different experience – it literally was two different companies."

Candice explained Ron's method of management with a respectful understanding: "He was the kind of man who wanted as much control as possible – over every element of OR *that was fun.*"

For Ron, Outdoor Research had been both a labor of love and a playground, and with his death the staff inherited much of the fun part of Ron Gregg's OR world. Candice explained that while the new paradigm didn't lessen the tragedy of losing Ron, it did change almost every aspect of life at the office.

DAN NORDSTROM EN ROUTE TO THE FIRST DESCENT OF MELAKWA POINT, SNOQUALMIE PASS, WASHINGTON.

Candice explained the new atmosphere at Outdoor Research like someone describing the difference between undergraduate studies and a masters program: "Everything that you'd ever felt as an employee – 'Wow, it would be great if we could do....' – OR had so much potential as a company. It did well but there was so much more that it could do, and it was like 'Wow, we're getting the opportunity to actually do this!' Dan would say 'Here is what I'd like to do. Here's where I'd like to be involved. Here's an idea. Go run with it. When we get close to the end, bring it back to me and we'll go from there.'"

With a nod to Ron's passion for the business, Candice concluded, "It was like a playground for us now all of a sudden."

Ironically, the new team managing Outdoor Research was designed in much the same way as the company's products had been designed for years – through adventures. But rather than wilderness adventures, it was adventures in business itself inspiring the change. With Dan's internal compass on the retail world, and the team's depth of experience, every roadblock was overcome with careful consideration and resulted in a more sophisticated design of the Outdoor Research business model. Within a few years, the company had exponentially exceeded both any previous year's sales and the most optimistic forecasts, and Outdoor Research was riding a wave of growth bigger than any time in the company's history.

What it takes to be successful in the mountains and what it takes to be successful in business have always been close cousins. In the days when huge expeditions conquered the biggest peaks by sheer numbers and endless supplies of equipment, successful businesses conquered the market through sheer production. Magazines overprinted so they could reach the next print run threshold that would allow them to demand more advertising dollars – and then just threw away the excess copies. Ski manufacturers built way more skis than they could sell, because factories worked more efficiently when they produced huge runs of the same thing rather than custom quantities of several different models. Other industries did the same thing. From automobile parts to jeans, unsold inventories were as common as fax machines. It was a wasteful time in both mountaineering and business.

In the mountains, when the glory of the summit attempt had passed, expeditions left ropes, tents, oxygen bottles and trash – and walked away. Climbers have learned that a leaner approach to mountaineering not only has less impact on the mountain, but also enables climbers to accomplish more during periods of stable weather and optimal conditions. A combination of technology and philosophy has made the small, self-sufficient team, once viewed as foolhardy, into what is commonly the safest and most effective way to climb a mountain.

In business, raw materials and energy are becoming so expensive, and competition so fierce, that only the leanest and most agile companies are thriving. Producing a solid product is no longer enough. The product needs to be desirable when viewed alongside the plethora of others on the market, and it needs to be produced in a customized, high-quality, low-waste method in order to compete. The days of climbing mountains at any cost – and of making products regardless of the waste produced – are over.

Dan Nordstrom's combined experience with both mountain adventure and business leadership in a global apparel company gave Outdoor Research a leader who would not only respect and build upon Ron Gregg's bombproof foundation, but also navigate the rough waters of modern business with world-class efficiency and methodology. The only remaining step was to take the Outdoor Research model global.

9 Verticulture

Scanning these myriad possibilities, with the appetite of a starving man perusing the pages of a gourmet magazine, I readily transformed the unknown to the known and I saw myself turning the hidden key that opened each new climb's secret and solved its mystery.

— Layton Kor, *Beyond the Vertical*

VERTFEST RANDO RACE BEGINS.
ALPENTAL SKI AREA, WASHINGTON.

After Clark Campbell's initial marathon vision quest in redesigning the Outdoor Research product line and production method, Dan Nordstrom's team began a quantum shift in the way the company's product design is orchestrated. To raise the bar of the adventure laboratory beyond Ron Gregg's high mark – not only in the financial sense but also in the significance of the company's contributions to the adventure world – was no small feat. Dan decided to keep the focus on design but to open the doors to the entire world to influence the design of the product as well as the management of the business. The concept was simple: rather than hire athletes or managers to advise on design and business strategy in an exclusive environment, the company would create a culture of inclusivity.

To achieve this, Dan borrowed some of the brightest elements from Ron's original business model. The Infinite Guarantee – if at any time an Outdoor Research product doesn't perform to a user's satisfaction, it will be replaced – was continued from the company's original lifetime warranty. Joe Wadden has been observing the Infinite Guarantee in action for 17 years: "I stop in to the OR retail store and overhear some customer say 'You guys just made my day!' I'll look over and see a ratty old pair of mitts on the counter. It happens over and over. The staff sees it as an opportunity."

At the core of the new inclusive culture at Outdoor Research is Dan Nordstrom's vast experience in the apparel industry combined with his own obsession with adventure. This means that suggestions by Outdoor Research customers and partners will be processed by a team that understands the idiosyncrasies of outdoor adventure as well as a team that can act quickly and effectively on a global scale. Orchestrating this transition to an inclusive design culture required several distinctly different strategies.

The first strategy was to invite users of Outdoor Research products to help in the design process through the unprecedented Lab Rat program, a web-based system where users are invited to review products in a format that turns the consumer into the designer. Many websites include reviews, but the Lab Rat interface is much more than a collection of reviews. It includes parameters customized to each product so that Lab Rat feedback can be most effectively collected and implemented by Outdoor Research's design team. Complete with the capability to upload contributors' avatars, the Lab Rat program essentially invites any outdoor enthusiast with computer access and a familiarity with Outdoor Research products to be part of the adrenaline laboratory started by Ron Gregg in 1981.

The second strategy was to get product into the hands of the people who used it hardest. In 1997 the American Mountain Guides Association, the AMGA, was accepted into the international guiding federation, the International Federation of Mountain Guides Associations, which oversees training standards and allows guides to practice their profession in other member countries. For Dan Nordstrom, who during his lifetime of adventure has watched guiding in North America go from an individually managed trade to an internationally regulated profession, the AMGA was an obvious gold mine for product design. To create a pipeline for feedback from guides, Outdoor Research began working with Martin Volken, a Swiss guide, and Margaret Wheeler, an American guide, to create an ongoing product-testing relationship between the AMGA and Outdoor Research.

The third strategy was to invite the retail stores and distribution network to help design not only Outdoor Research products but also the business model. To do this, Dan hit the road and visited many of the company's most loyal buyers. He asked them what they wanted to see different from Outdoor Research, and then went home and made it happen. One of his stops was in Tucson to talk to Dave Baker, the founder of the Summit Hut, one of the first outdoor specialty stores in America when Dave started it with some help from his parents while he was still a senior in high school in 1969.

Dave explained how timely Dan's visit had been: "Between vendors and retailers there's a synergy that has to happen. Under the last years of Ron's tenure, we were unsure of the opportunities with OR."

When Dan took the time to travel around the country in order to see what issues were facing retailers like the Summit Hut, it gave Dave renewed hope for the industry and for his store's relationship with Outdoor Research. Dave explained to Dan that what his store needed from OR came down to three things: a more interesting product line; flexibility in terms of special offers to spark excitement; and for Outdoor Research to engage smaller specialty retailers like the Summit Hut just as excitedly as bigger buyers.

"Much to my delight," says Dave, "Dan started to execute on all of these issues within a matter of months. We were invited to give proposals about how we would like to participate in OR, we had a chance to be part of OR's image on the worldwide web, and the new OR product designs and presentation of the products were really strong.

"For vendors, one of the trickiest things to do is to figure out how to share their bounty with retail partners, and Dan really got that right. He gave up a lot in terms of margins, inventory etc. But I think it paid off for him in the end.

"A lot has been written about how companies should do that, but it's not often executed – and Dan did it."

The fourth strategy was to invest in the backcountry community. In 1981, there was not a single event organized around backcountry skiing, rock climbing, boating or mountaineering. By 2011, organized gatherings of the adventure culture had become common venues for the newest techniques and most desirable products to gain a foothold in the industry. Climbing competitions, informal free-skiing competitions, film festivals and com-

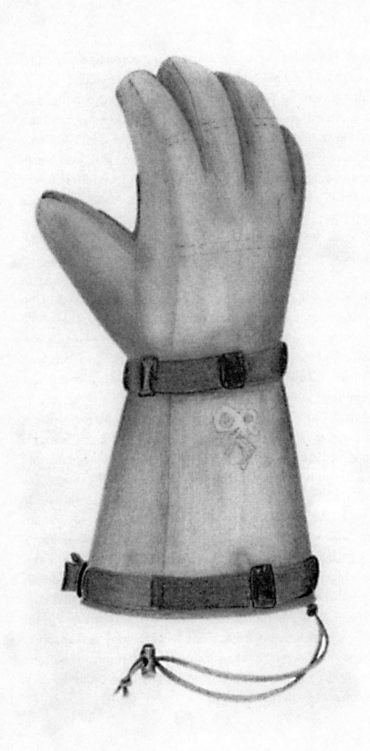

munity events dedicated to preserving and respecting natural resources have become a mainstay of the adventure culture.

To tap into the viral gold mine of shared psyche that can be found at these events, Outdoor Research sponsored a backcountry ski festival dubbed Vertfest, held at the Alpental ski area near Snoqualmie Pass. Similar festivals are popping up all over North America, modeled roughly, with a more irreverent western flavor, after the big rando races that have become extremely popular in Europe over the last decade. "Rando" is short for the French term *randonnée*, the ski technology also called alpine touring, or AT, that allows the ski boot heels to be released for hiking up hill, and then locked down for the descent like a regular alpine binding. In Europe, the big rando races are nearly as popular as World Cup ski racing, complete with audiences four people deep lining the racecourse, ringing cowbells and cheering for their favorite racers. Many of the top rando athletes are former Nordic racers with the cardiovascular capacity of whales and ski heritage going back generations.

Turn for turn, Alpental is one of the most exciting ski areas in North America, with only a single, short beginner run, a couple of intermediate runs, and a mountain laced with chutes, cliffs and steeper terrain than you'll find in-bounds at most ski resorts. The upper chairlift ends on a rocky dome more akin to a summit in the backcountry than the top of a ski area. The in-bounds ski runs blend with spectacular backcountry ski terrain including formidable rocky spires, narrow chutes, big faces and complicated, corniced ridges. As far as the eye can see, everything appears skiable – for somebody.

The original plan for the ski resort, hanging on the wall in the base lodge, included twice as many lifts accessing perhaps three times as much terrain as the current Alpental resort. If the complete area had been developed it would have been by far the most extreme ski area in the country.

On race day the intimidating ski area was cloaked in mists that clung to the big cliffs and swirled through the old-growth trees lining the edges of the runs. In the US and Canada there are a handful of skiers who take rando racing seriously, but the vast majority of participants at North American rando races are average backcountry skiers wanting to expand their own horizons in the sport they love. Of the 120 people who lined up at the starting line of the Vertfest race, perhaps only half a dozen were really competing for the win. The rest wore various kinds of randonnée and telemark gear and many of them carried stuffed animals strapped to their packs in honor of Monika Johnson, a local ski hero who died tragically the week before the race when a cornice collapsed under her during a ski tour in the Cascades.

The race climbs the 2,200-foot mountain along a scenic route past giant cedar trees and frozen ice pillars. On the rocky upper part, the course follows narrow couloirs where the skiers were forced to remove their skis to climb the steepest sections directly under the exposed Edelweiss chairlift.

At first glance, the racecourse looks like the most suicidal downhill on earth. Gates are set up at wide intervals, often near the edge of cliffs or in thick forest at the edge of the ski runs. But the gates mark the uphill part of the course. Nobody in a stable frame of mind would try to run the course backwards at top speed.

At the top, the skiers remove their skins, the adhesive-backed strips that allow a skier to walk up steep hills without slipping, and drop into the steep, bumpy and infamous ski run called International. One skier said at the finish line while he rubbed his thighs with a grimace on his face: "That downhill killed my quads. I'm an uphill guy, really. I wish the race ended on the top."

Surprisingly, rando races are won or lost on the downhill. The top competitors are all veritable lungs on skis, so the frontrunners end up on top at the same time, strip their skins off in a matter of seconds and then charge the downhill with abandon. The elite racers run two laps on the 2,200-vertical-foot Alpental course and finish in less than two hours. One racer described the course with a single word: steep.

The course setter, Martin Volken, a local mountain guide, Outdoor Research ambassador and Swiss expat, explained that his very strategy in designing the course was to make it friendly for the spectators and exciting for the racers. "I wanted the race to be strenuous but inspiring," he explained. "I want the event to be two things: number one, a gathering of the backcountry community; and number two, an inspiration to the lift skiers. If the race can inspire even one (downhill) skier to try out the backcountry or even get in a bit better shape, then it was a success."

For Martin, after spending a lifetime in the mountains, the more hedonistic elements of the sport hold little interest. In a conversation over a coffee in the Alpental base lodge amidst the clomping of ski boots and the shrill laughter of happy skiers, Martin revealed a passion for community that is rare among even the most committed natives. He revealed clearly why he is an ideal spokesman for Outdoor Research's new paradigm of inclusivity: "The last thing I want to do is sit around and talk about how steep I skied yesterday. It's all about the aspiration element. This may sound weird coming from a Swiss guy, but I'm trying to popularize American ski mountaineering."

Martin runs his mountain and ski guiding business, Pro Guiding Service, and retail shop out of North Bend, a sleepy town snuggled against the western escarpment of the Cascades at the foot of Snoqualmie Pass. With easy access to great skiing and summertime recreation, he says, "It's a great place to live." Then added, "If you don't consider the weather."

In North Bend, Martin has become a community leader. He explained that the town sidestepped the real estate craze of the 1990s by disallowing large-scale developments, and while the nearby National Forest is home to some of the most popular hiking trails in Washington, the public land in the state does not have a tradition of wilderness access like California, Utah and Colorado. There are no hut systems, and several trails have been closed because of lack of federal funding for maintenance. Now, as a business owner, Martin participates in planning meetings for the community of North Bend, and he sees the chance to influence the future of public policy.

With proactive cooperation from the Alpental ski area and the town of North Bend, and sponsorship from Outdoor Research, Martin has a powerful combination of entities to help shape the event as he sees fit. "The Pro (Ski) Patrol really wants this (Vertfest) to happen." He explained, "My hat is off to those guys." The ski patrol used a snowcat to create a snow bridge across an open stream, stationed patrollers near the race to alert downhill skiers, and gave the premium space at the base area to the event so the downhill skiers could also experience this adventurous new aspect of skiing culture.

The management at Alpental stepped behind Vertfest immediately. As a ski area where patrollers are still allowed to have facial hair and duct-tape patches on their ski pants, it is the kind of place where backcountry skiers feel comfortable – in fact welcome. With little else besides steep and aggressive terrain, and gated access to the surrounding backcountry, the ski area management and patrol take a progressive approach to backcountry use. The area recently opened a new backcountry gate, and Alpental marketing director Guy Lawrence enthusiastically described the trend he sees in backcountry use: "We see exponentially more people going out of the gate every year."

The first day of Vertfest included a ski demo, clinics, and a film festival in North Bend. The ski clinics included sidecountry steeps classes for men and women, skinning technique and an avalanche terrain selection clinic.

Margaret Wheeler led the women's sidecountry steeps clinic.

Her class began at the Alpental base area, where she asked the six women if they had ever rappelled or used an ice axe with skis on. A couple of hands went up. This was no group of trophy wives enrolled in Margaret's clinic to impress their husbands. One of them was a long-time guest of Margaret's who had skied the legendary Haute Route from Chamonix to Zermatt. These were women who, while not superstars of ski media, in many ways represented the true modern face of adventure skiing.

The lesson began at the top of International, where thousands of pairs of skis had polished the entrance slope into a 50-degree sheet of ice. Margaret began by having the group sideslip down the ice and traverse across out of the way of other skiers. Then she began a series of exercises designed to develop a more aggressive stance and quiet the upper body. Between periods of expert instruction Margaret kept the tone lighthearted. When she noticed one of the women getting the hang of a new technique Margaret yelled, "Yeah, Dianne, you're getting it! I can see your tongue!"

After a couple of runs on International, everyone in the clinic seemed to be enjoying the steeps as well as Margaret's sense of humor, and one of the participants who had just fallen in love with steep skiing said, "Who knew what a difference a run can make!"

With Outdoor Research ambassadors helping more people fall in love with the backcountry, and senior management openly developing feedback systems for backcountry users to be a part of product development, Ron Gregg's company has regained its place as a mainstay of the adventure culture.

As of the 30th anniversary of Outdoor Research, in 2011, the company is combining these three strategies into a global system of relationships based on valuing feedback from every corner of the planet. This means utilizing the Lab Rat program to learn

OUTDOOR RESEARCH AMBASSADOR ZACH GIFFIN FLUFFING HIS PILLOW, MT. BAKER, WASHINGTON.

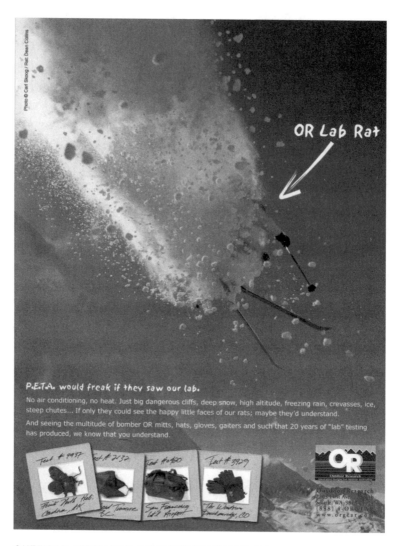

OUTDOOR RESEARCH ADVERTISEMENT FROM THE EARLY 2000s.

from adventurers in different places, maintaining open communication with retailers and distributors worldwide to ensure their specialized needs are considered in how Outdoor Research does business, and promoting inclusive outdoor events to stay in intimate contact with adventure cultures all over the globe.

Ron would be happy to know that what he wrote about value in the 1996 Outdoor Research catalog is just as applicable today as it was the day he penned it:

> At OR we put an enormous amount of effort into producing these products as efficiently as possible so they can be priced just as low as possible. Our production plant here in Seattle is modern, mechanized, organized and computerized. Our production people are highly skilled, highly motivated and hard working. We deal directly with our dealers so there are no distributors in the middle. And those of us running the show spend our vacations hiking, camping, climbing, biking, sailing and pursuing other relatively cheap but healthful pursuits rather than gambling in Vegas or hobnobbing with the jet-setters in the Bahamas!

Ron would be thrilled to know that Dalisay Detorres is still manager of the day shift at the Outdoor Research factory; that the staff could walk up to his old office overlooking the Seattle skyline and talk directly to the owner of the company as they always had; that the apparel line is the fastest-growing branch of the company; and that the brand's position as the quality innovation standard in the outdoor industry is as solid as at any time in the last 30 years.

The story of the last three decades of Outdoor Research and the outdoor industry raises the question of what will happen next. With a recreational class emerging in places like China, Brazil and India, and the outdoor recreation market's proven resilience during difficult economic periods, the future of the company and

OUTDOOR RESEARCH AMBASSADOR EMILIE DRINKWATER
SPORTING MANY LAYERS OF MODERN COMFORT IN THE GUNKS,
NEW YORK.

the industry is exciting. As of 2011, Outdoor Research's fastest-growing markets are in Chile, China, Japan, Australia and New Zealand.

Clark Campbell explained what is perhaps the company's simplest recipe for success in new markets: "We make it really easy for them to buy our products, with factory-direct delivery. And we're one of the only ones left that is privately held, so it frees us to try things and it puts a face on the company that retailers and factories really like."

While the sweet smell of success has been thick in the Outdoor Research offices, at the same time, the challenges facing the company and the industry are complex. With the proliferation of Internet shopping, some retail stores are struggling; yet the retail experience remains a crucial part of the equation, and stores that adjust to the new paradigm are not only making a profit but have the opportunity to become valuable cultural centers for adventure sports.

Another issue facing the industry is that cutting-edge design can be copied so quickly that competing brands are making products that look painfully similar, and brand differentiation is becoming cloudy. Dave Baker, who has spent more years in the outdoor retail business than almost anyone, shared his concerns about the new face of outdoor product design, as well as his hope for the future. "I personally am getting bored," he explained. "It's not that these companies are bad – they're great – it's just that I'm bored. What I'm seeing from the outside is strong evidence that much of the design is now happening in Asia, and designs have gotten homogeneous as a result. I'm particularly interested when vendors find a way to have their designs stand out."

To meet the new challenges, the goal of letting adventure – rather than competitors' products – dictate design remains a powerful directive. Ron Gregg would roll over in his grave and laugh heartily to know that 30 years after he started the company, the business would be quickly addressing the suggestions of its partner companies, and that the designs of Outdoor Research products would be inspired not by the adventures of a single master designer, but through a global network of Outdoor Research customers having the opportunity to contribute the lessons of their own adventures to the design.

Hanging on a tree deep in the backcountry of the Pacific Northwest there is a sign that once marked a parking space at 2203 1st Avenue South in Seattle. Rust is sneaking in around the edges, but it still reads "Ron Gregg Parking Only."

At the parking space where the sign used to be, in front of the Outdoor Research factory store, adventurers of all sorts can be found. Sea kayakers park there while they run in to buy a sunhat that will shed the rain on their way to a paddle in the San Juan Islands. Mountaineers park there to pick up the latest waterproof and breathable shell before heading to the Himalaya. Rock climbers park there while they try on some climbing pants that will make those Yosemite high steps just a little bit easier. Skiers park there to grab a pair of gloves to stay dry and warm on a deep-powder binge in British Columbia.

All of these people parking in Ron's old spot have one thing in common: they make space in their lives for adventure. Perhaps the most lasting legacy of Ron Gregg, and the adventure culture he helped shape, is not technical innovation only, but making adventure a way of life. Ron may have had a rough edge in the design room, but when one of his employees approached him to see if he could take three weeks off to go kayaking in Tonga, Ron replied, "Three weeks to go kayaking in Tonga? That's hardly enough!"

Acknowledgements

In many ways this book is thanks to the entire outdoor community: the climbers, the hikers, the skiers, the boaters, the cyclists, the runners, the dirt bags, the weekend warriors, the beginners, the veterans and everyone else who participates in the outdoor sports that bring so much health, so many thrills and so many great friends into so many people's lives.

Then additional thanks are due to all the people who have helped make Outdoor Research a brand that embodies the adventures that enrich our days on this diverse planet: the people who have worked in the Outdoor Research factory and offices, the families who accommodated both the adventures in business and the adventures in the wilderness, and the adventure and business associates who have helped spread the passion and the brand all over the world.

The names of all the people who deserve thanks would fill a book, but the first name on the list is Randy King. Randy was the steadfast second in command who allowed the founder of Outdoor Research, Ron Gregg, to obsess over adventure-driven design for nearly 25 years. Then, when I began work on this book, Randy took the time to share photos, check facts and devote a little more of his life to this story long after he'd already had enough of it.

My own path to the telling of this story began in 2008 while skiing in blower powder in the backcountry near Revelstoke, British Columbia. One of the other skiers was calling a tall telemark skier named Dan "Mr. OR." Mr. OR? I wondered. I'd started using Outdoor Research gear like so many people during the 80s, when the brand was the only game in town when it came to gaiters and gloves that worked well in the backcountry. I had heard of Ron Gregg, and thought surely this younger tele skier wasn't *the* Mr. OR.

As it turned out, Dan Nordstrom is the current owner of the company and is indeed *the* Mr. OR. The man I had been thinking of was *Dr.* OR, aka Ron Gregg, the legendary and self-proclaimed "gear guy" who was the mind behind the design powerhouse of Outdoor Research during the 80s and 90s. It was Dan who invited me to author this book, and it is thanks to him that I have the honor of bringing the adventure-filled story of Outdoor Research to the world.

While researching this book, I crisscrossed Seattle with Hollywood-blue skies as a backdrop to the postcard skyline, and also drove through rush hour with water pouring from the skies with such force that "rain" is hardly the right word to describe the deluge. Sharon Gregg, Ron's widow, described the phenomenon as "impressionistic driving," and I thank her for what was surely an emotional dinner conversation about Ron. His brother and sisters, Bob, Laurie and Lana, and his brother-in-law, Dave Nicol, are also due hearty thanks.

Lance Young, one of Ron's closest friends, and Rebecca Wallick were instrumental in sorting out of some of the wildest adventures chronicled in this book. Dan Cauthorn, Martin Volken, Margaret Wheeler, Dave Baker, Carlos Buhler and Gordy Skoog all shared their perspective as seasoned explorers.

Karl Kohagen, Candice Springstead, Ted Steudel, Kaj Bune, Tim Davis, the late Carl Skoog, Eric Cleaveland and Bill Hartlieb all contributed to this story with their rich experience over the last few decades.

Joe Wadden, Ammi Borenstein, Clark Campbell, Christian Folk, Eric Leung, Jerry Gundersen, Troy Jones, Alek Kutches, Dalisay Detorres, Lauren O'Connell-Fujii and Jeremy Park took time away from the current rapidly growing world of Outdoor Research to contribute to this book.

Audrey Hicks, Jordan Wand and Charles Lozner kept me on track and provided patient support during the creative process. My uncle, Kevin Cremin, and his family put up with my chaotic schedule and opened their home to me throughout my research in Seattle.

The Alpental ski area and Vertfest gave me a glimpse into the future of skiing. Aaron Clifford and his research on the history of Outdoor Research gave me an excellent background to the story. Castle Rock in Boulder Canyon provided much-needed respite from the keyboard, and its sandbag climbs kept me sane during this project.

Lastly, I'd like to thank my wife for taking time away from her own career to advise me in every element of my own, my twin son and daughter for understanding that my work time equals their pizza, and my own adventure partners who've shared the thousands of pitches, turns, adventures, laughs, cries, screams and whispers that make up the best days of my life.

Photographs